STUDENT ACTIVITY BOOK FOR

My People

Abba Eban's
History of the Jews
VOLUME II

ADAPTED BY DAVID BAMBERGER

by
Morris J. Sugarman

BEHRMAN HOUSE, INC., PUBLISHERS
NEW YORK, NEW YORK

Acknowledgments

I would like to say thank you to several people whose help on this activity book has been invaluable: Adam Bengal, managing editor of Behrman House, who supervised its production with patience, firmness, and skill; Karen Rossel, who read the original manuscript, and made so many improvements; and Ms. Marva R. Hilliard, who did her usual fine and professional job of typing the manuscript.

And of course, my special thanks to Seymour Rossel, who oversaw the entire project and whose contributions to it went well beyond the realm of editing.

ISBN: 0-87441-333-8

1 2 3 4 5 86 85 84 83 82 81

Book designed and illustrated by Marvin Friedman

Dedication
For Lianna, with all my love.

Contents

STUDENT ACTIVITY BOOK FOR

My People

Abba Eban's
History of the Jews
VOLUME II

Chapter 1

THE WORLD IN 1776

A JEWISH TRAVEL DIARY—1776*

An imaginary traveler left us this record of places of Jewish interest in 1776. Using the map on pages 16–17 of the textbook (and the illustration on page 18), identify the places on the blank line following each entry from the travel log.

1. "Although this is not the city of Moses Mendelssohn, it is an important center of German Jewish life. There are many great synagogues and places of learning. And, believe me, the Jews here are feeling the same changes in their lives as are the Jews in the capital."

_____

2. "Incredible! Right in the middle of Africa! Black Jews that look exactly like their non-Jewish neighbors. And they say that they come from the children of King Solomon and the Queen of Sheba!"

_____

3. "Sometimes I am so sentimental. Here, I took the earth and rubbed it in my hand. I found a small synagogue and prayed with Jews in this city of David. And I kept remembering the words of the prophet Isaiah: 'From out of Zion shall go forth the Law.'"

_____

4. "For this Jewish community, the event of a lifetime—in fact, the greatest event of several lifetimes—has taken place in

*Answers to starred exercises may be found in the answer key at the end of the book.

this year of 1776. They have had a front-row seat as the Declaration of Independence was signed."

_____

5. "It should have been no surprise. After all, Jews have lived in this country for centuries. Still, it was a shock to see a Jewish community—ghetto and all—so close to the Vatican, the center of Catholicism."

_____

6. "This synagogue, the first in New York, could be nicknamed 'Seixas' triumph.' Of course, Seixas took a great gamble here; and, if things had gone the other way, it would have been known as 'Seixas' folly.'"

_____

7. "Everywhere you go in this city, people speak of the brilliant mind of Moses Mendelssohn. Thanks to Mr. Mendelssohn, this city will no doubt become famous as the place where Jews stepped into the modern world."

_____

8. "Here I was privileged to visit Rabbi Shneur Zalman. He spoke to me in the most moving manner, calling for the unity of the Jews. No wonder this country is gaining a reputation as one of the great centers of Jewish learning in Eastern Europe."

_____

THE REASONS WHY

In your own words, complete the following sentences:

1. Mendelssohn decided to translate the Torah into German because

2. Shneur Zalman worried about the new political and social freedoms that Jews were gaining in the West because

3. The Declaration of Independence was particularly important to the Jews because

4. The Enlightenment is known as the Age of Reason because

5. The Enlightenment posed a serious threat to the ruling classes because

FIND THE OUTSIDER*

Each of the statements below is correct, except for one section. Find the "outsider" section and circle the letter before it.

1. The Enlightenment   (a) was a challenge to long-standing religious and political beliefs;   (b) encouraged scientific thinking and experimentation;   (c) was a time when all books not based on the scientific method were banned or burned;   (d) laid the groundwork for breaking down the ghetto walls that had separated Jews and non-Jews for so long.

2. The Declaration of Independence   (a) was the final step in the long argument and the many disputes between the New World colonists and the British Empire;   (b) guaranteed that the United States would be forever free of racial and religious injustice;   (c) established the principle, for the first time among nations, that people had the right to make their own laws and create their own government;   (d) claimed that kings and nobles did not rule by divine right, and had no special pipeline to God.

3. The map of the Diaspora (pages 16–17 in the text) shows that   (a) most Jewish communities in the United States were set up in coastal cities;   (b) Jewish life was unable to sustain itself and survive in faraway backward lands;   (c) there were Jews living in Israel in the eighteenth century;   (d) most Jews lived in Europe in the eighteenth century.

4. The story of Gershom Seixas teaches that   (a) Jewish settlers in the New World were willing from the start to be part of the movement for American independence;   (b) not all Jews agreed that a break with Great Britain was the wisest course of action;   (c) a number of Jews saw a link between the struggle of Americans for freedom, and the Jewish struggle for freedom;   (d) the Jews in England paid a harsh price for the actions of Seixas and his followers.

5. Moses Mendelssohn   (a) sought freedom for the Jews because of his bitter memories of prejudice and hatred;   (b) believed that the future held even more freedom for the Jews than they had known in centuries;   (c) worried that the Jews of the ghetto would not understand or be able to live in the outside world;   (d) took steps to prepare the Jews of his time for their entry into modern life.

6. Rabbi Shneur Zalman   (a) worried that the new freedom for Jews in the West would weaken the fabric of traditional Jewish life;   (b) believed in, and worked toward, Jewish unity;   (c) taught that scholarship was evil because it destroyed the Jew's ability to pray;   (d) faced bitter opposition from traditional Jews who rejected Hasidism.

IDEA SCRAMBLE*

Beside each of the circles below is a set of words trying to become an idea. Unscramble the words and write the ideas in the circles to complete the "Wheel of Enlightenment."

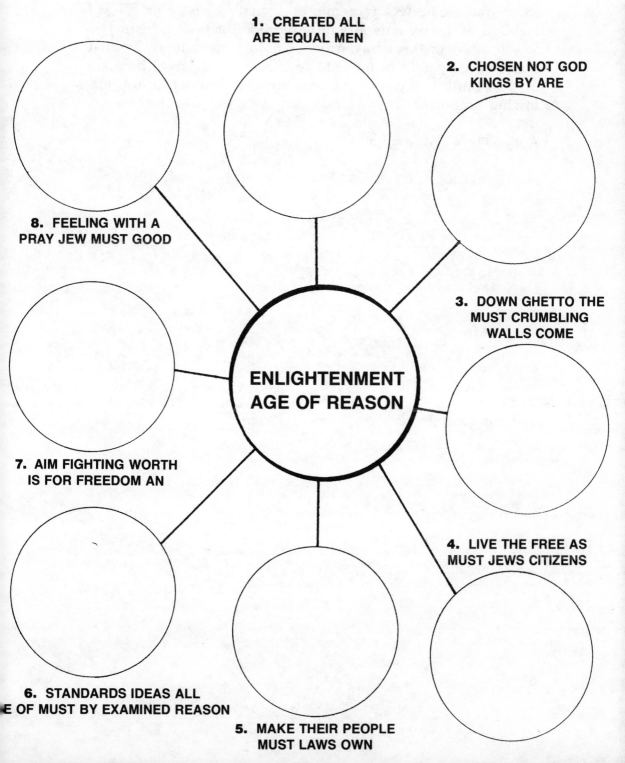

1. CREATED ALL ARE EQUAL MEN

2. CHOSEN NOT GOD KINGS BY ARE

8. FEELING WITH A PRAY JEW MUST GOOD

3. DOWN GHETTO THE MUST CRUMBLING WALLS COME

ENLIGHTENMENT AGE OF REASON

7. AIM FIGHTING WORTH IS FOR FREEDOM AN

4. LIVE THE FREE AS MUST JEWS CITIZENS

**6. STANDARDS IDEAS ALL
E OF MUST BY EXAMINED REASON**

5. MAKE THEIR PEOPLE MUST LAWS OWN

THEN AND TODAY

WHAT IS A GOOD JEW?

The chapter makes the point that, "Even two centuries ago there was not perfect agreement on what makes 'a good Jew.' ... One of the reasons for studying modern Jewish history is ... to discover the many ways of being 'good Jews.'" What does being a good Jew mean to you now? What part of Judaism do you think is the most important? Try completing the following statement:

A good Jew is one who

Chapter 2

AT THE ENDS OF THE EARTH

WHO, OR WHAT, AM I?*

1. My husband and I are the rulers of Spain, generally praised as the royal sponsors of Columbus, who can also boast of driving several hundred thousand Jews from their homes. My name is _____

2. I am what is left of the ancient Temple of Jerusalem. I stand as a symbol of both grief and hope, and am a place of prayer for Jews. Since the Six Day War in 1967, I have also become the symbol of a united Jerusalem. I am the _____.

3. I was trained as a rabbi, but my proudest achievements have been in building, farming, road construction, city planning, and synagogue architecture—all in Eretz Yisrael. And I did all this nearly a century and a half before the first Zionist pioneers came to the Holy Land. I am _____.

4. I am the man on the spot. I wanted no part of this rag-tag band of refugees, but my superiors who sit comfortably in their offices in the old country, gave in to Jewish pressure, allowing these people to settle here. My name is _____.

5. I am a rabbi from Safed. My greatest work was the *Shulchan Aruch,* a guide to Jewish law. My name is _____.

6. I am the Hebrew word meaning both "justice" and "righteousness" that describes the support given by Jews of the Diaspora to the Jewish community of Palestine. I am

_____

7

7. As a Jewish immigrant from Poland, I was privileged to raise vast sums of money for the American cause during the Revolutionary War. I am _____.

8. Many said I was "pushy," a "troublemaker" who could not leave well enough alone. But I believe that we must take on the job of self-defense, rather than leaving our protection to the will and whim of others. And I think that is one of the principles of equality and independence—and of Zionism, too. I am _____.

9. Strange! Despite the history of hatred toward my people, and the fact that Jews were barred by law on penalty of death from crossing the ocean, I was the first European to touch the shores of the New World. My name is _____.

10. I am the American president who publicly proclaimed the unparalleled contribution of the Jewish people to human civilization. I am _____.

INSIGHTS IN DEPTH

Support each of the following general statements with a reference to, or a quotation from, the chapter in the textbook. (You can refer to the text, the photographs, the illustrations, and the special topic.)

1. Being a victim of religious persecution is no guarantee that a person will be free of religious prejudice.

_____

_____

_____

2. At times, positive personalities or events in general history have been sources of hatred, suffering, tragedy, and destruction in Jewish history.

_____

_____

_____

3. The beliefs and ideals of the American Revolution strengthened the position of Jews in the United States.

_____

_____

_____

WORD SCRAMBLE*

Each scrambled word is an experience or quality shared by the small, struggling communities living in both the New World and Eretz Yisrael during the years covered by the chapter. Sometimes these experiences contradicted each other, but then a person can have a good day and a bad day in the same week. Unscramble the words. Write them in the boxes. Then, unscramble the circled letters to make one word that was a vision in both the New World and Eretz Yisrael.

1. JERDIPECU

2. ROTEPENICUS

3. SPHARDIH

4. MOIRYNIT

5. SNIRDEFIPH

6. GRENASTINDUND

9

MAP STUDY

JEWS ON THE MOVE*

This chapter deals mainly with Jews on the move in the United States and Eretz Yisrael. Each number on the map below is a key location discussed in the chapter. Using the descriptions (with matching numbers) below, write the name of each location beside its number on the map.

1. The first Jewish community in the Americas.

2. The Dutch colony that received the first Jewish settlers to come to what is now the United States.

3. An American colony, originally settled by religious people escaping persecution, that for a long time refused to allow Jews to settle there.

4. The body of water with islands that offered refuge to Jews fleeing from the Portuguese armies in South America.

5. The port city in which Jews received a letter from George Washington.

6. The famous port of Israel built on a mountain where, in the story of Elijah, the Jews were slaughtered by invading Crusaders.

7. The city of David, site of the Western Wall.

8. The center of Jewish intellectual life in Eretz Yisrael after the Turkish conquest, where Joseph Karo wrote the *Shulchan Aruch*.

9. An ancient port city that served as a center for French and English rabbis and scholars during the thirteenth century.

10. The ancient city where once the Sanhedrin met and the Jerusalem Talmud was completed, was rebuilt by Rabbi Haim Abulafia in the eighteenth century.

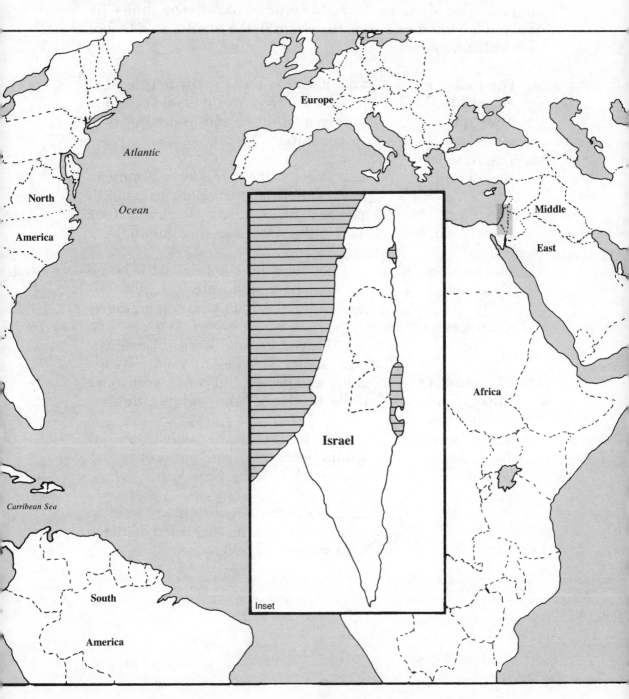

EVENTS AND EFFECTS*

Match the events in the left column with the effects they helped bring about in the right column. Make your choice by placing the number before the event in the blank space before the matching effect.

1. The independence of Holland from Spain

2. The American Revolution

3. The efforts of Haym Salomon

4. The tradition of Tzedakah

5. Asser Levy's victory

6. The story of the Muslim sheik of Northern Palestine and Rabbi Haim Abulafia

_____ Established the principle that Jews in the New World would be equal in responsibilities and in privileges of citizenship.

_____ Proof that many American Jews—often at great personal, political, and financial risk—actively took part in the American Revolution.

_____ Showed that the Jews of the world maintained their loyalty to Eretz Yisrael and to the Jews who settled there.

_____ Proved that the Jews of Eretz Yisrael did not have to limit themselves to study and prayer, but could work to rebuild the Holy Land and its cities.

_____ Started a trickle, which one day would become a steady flow, of Jewish immigration to the New World.

_____ Made the equal rights of Jews in this country a firm, ingrained, national idea supported by law.

Chapter 3

IN THE HEARTLAND OF OUR PEOPLE

TRUE OR FALSE?*   (T) (F)

1. Jews originally immigrated to Poland because of the terrible anti-Semitism in the rest of Europe.   T   F

2. Jacob Frank was the first in a long line of false Messiahs to plague the Jewish people.   T   F

3. Poland's political problems in the eighteenth century caused suffering for the Jews in Poland and made them feel insecure.   T   F

4. Mendelssohn's experiences were dramatic proof that the greater a Jew's acceptance into Gentile society, the weaker the ties to his or her tradition and people.   T   F

5. Jacob Frank's ideas appealed to Christian religious and political leaders mainly because of their anti-Jewish bent.
                                                                T   F

6. Three of the major reasons that some Jews became followers of false Messiahs were poverty, powerlessness, and little or no Jewish education.   T   F

7. Mendelssohn's successes and prestige stirred Christian society to view Judaism in a favorable new light.   T   F

8. "Frederick the Great" was a dictator whose tyranny and oppression knew no bounds.   T   F

9. Many Court Jews tried to use their privileges and influence to make life better for the Jewish people.   T   F

10. The Hasidim and Mitnagdim bitterly opposed each other, each group calling the other "nonbelievers."   T   F

11. Because of the chain of political problems that overtook Poland in the eighteenth century, that tortured country produced little in the areas of fine arts and crafts.   T   F

12. Not all Polish Jews were confined to the shtetl; a number of Jews lived in Poland's big cities.   T   F

HUNTING HIDDEN WORDS*

In the maze of letters that follows are hidden the transliterations of seven Hebrew words that appear in chapters two and three of the textbook. They may be written vertically, horizontally, or diagonally; at the beginning of a line or in its middle; and may even be creeping around a corner. Some even may share a letter. Circle the hidden words. To help you, here are seven clues.

1. The spokesman for the Jewish community before Christian authorities.

2. The name of the founder of Hasidism, which, translated from Hebrew, means "the owner of a good name."

3. Charity, which is the Hebrew word for both "justice" and "righteousness."

4. A Jewish marriage contract, from the Hebrew word meaning "to write."

5. The name of the Jewish Supreme Court in ancient times.

6. The group of traditionalists that fought against the Hasidim, from the Hebrew word meaning "against" or "opposed."

7. The title given to Elijah of Vilna because of his scholarship and wisdom. The word itself means "genius."

```
S M K O N Z B A A L
A H E C T X F K P S
N X T Z E D A K A H
H M U A P C L Z T E
E R B A D G H G P M
D T A P T L W A Z T
R A H M I V A O E O
I F I G U E H N X V
N L A R Q U A D F G
M I T N A G D I M C
```

LOOKING FOR UNDERSTANDING

The questions below offer crucial keys to understanding the explosive developments of eighteenth century Jewish life in Europe. Answer them briefly and clearly.

1. How would you explain the powerful attraction to some Jews of such false Messiahs as Shabbetai Zevi and Jacob Frank?

_____

_____

_____

2. Why were Christian leaders so anxious for Moses Mendelssohn to abandon Judaism and convert to Christianity?

_____

_____

_____

3. What were the key ingredients of Ḥasidism's message to the Jewish people?

_____

_____

_____

4. What reasons can you give for the bitter and passionate fight of the Mitnagdim against the Ḥasidim?

_____

_____

_____

5. In what way were modern ideas from Central Europe a common enemy to both Ḥasidim and Mitnagdim?

_____

_____

_____

THEN AND TODAY

ACHING NEEDS

As the chapter points out, Shabbetai Zevi and Jacob Frank were not accidents of history. They became popular because they seemed to answer deep and aching needs of the Jews of their time. Can you point to aching needs, conditions of hardship and suffering, in our own time that could result in bringing modern false Messiahs to power and popularity?

Chapter 4

THE AGE OF REVOLUTION

WHO, WHAT, WHERE, AND WHEN AM I?*

1. I am a ghetto. Shakespeare wrote about me in a play about Jewish merchants. Napoleon ended my isolation in 1797. _____

2. I was conquered by Napoleon, but the weather of my country forced Napoleon and his army to retreat. _____

3. I am the book, coauthored by a man of Jewish birth, that proclaims the unity of the workers of the world, and urges workers to pool their strength and to take the political and economic power that is rightly theirs. _____

4. I am the country to which many poor and struggling European workers migrated, after their revolutions and uprisings failed to produce positive changes. _____

5. I am the famous military battle in which Napoleon suffered his final defeat (even my name has come to mean "defeat"). _____

6. No people or country ever went to war in my name, yet I am considered as much a revolution as the American and French revolutions. _____

7. I am a political philosophy that became popular in the nineteenth century after the defeat of Napoleon. My major idea can be summed up in a single word: uniqueness. I teach that each people has its unique history, language, culture, and destiny. _____

8. I am a philosophy that grew out of the sufferings of the industrial revolution. My main point is that the people themselves must control the means of production and distribution. I can flourish in either a dictatorship or a democracy; my major concern is economic equality. _____

THE REASONS WHY

In your own words, complete the following statements:

1. The French Revolution was far more violent and far less permanent than the American Revolution because

2. Napoleon was able to seize power in France because

3. Nationalism swept over Europe in the nineteenth century because

4. The rise of industrialism is called a revolution because

IDEA SCRAMBLE*

Unscramble the groups of words in the circles below to reveal some of the ideas that rumbled through Europe in the late eighteenth and early nineteenth centuries. Write the unscrambled sentences on the lines to the right of each circle. (The ideas may contradict one another—Europe was, after all, a place of conflict.)

1.
OBSOLETE
IS OF
GOVERNMENT
THE FORM AN
MONARCHY

_____

_____

2.
PEOPLE
PLACE BE THEIR
REBELLIOUS
PUT COMMON
THE IN
MUST

_____

_____

3.
BECOME
EMPIRE
EUROPE A
CAN
UNITED

_____

_____

4.
SPECIAL A
NATION
EVERY
CHARACTER
HAS

_____

_____

5.

BE SKILLED MACHINES BY CRAFTSMEN REPLACED WILL

_____

_____

6.

GOVERNMENT RIGHT THE CONSTITUTIONAL HAVE PEOPLE TO THE

_____

_____

7.

MAKE CAN INDUSTRY IT RIGHT PROFIT A MUCH AS PRIVATE HAS TO AS

_____

_____

8.

CONTROL MEANS THE PRODUCTION MUST WORKERS OF THE

_____

_____

A MIXED BAG

The chapter stresses that historical events are often a mixed bag of both positive and negative effects. The French Revolution, for example, was ablaze with noble ideas such as "Liberty! Equality! Fraternity!," yet it also turned into a blood bath.

Each of the diagrams below represents a historical development discussed in the chapter. On the positive side, put down what you think are the best or most promising things about that development. On the negative side, list what you think are the worst or most destructive features. (You can leave a blank if you think an event had no positive or negative side.)

1. Nationalism	
Positive	**Negative**

2. Democracy	
Positive	**Negative**

3. The Industrial Revolution	
Positive	**Negative**

4.	The Revolutions of 1848
Positive	**Negative**

THEN AND TODAY

HOW IS ZIONISM DIFFERENT?

The special topic on "isms" (page 45 of the text) states that modern Zionism is a nationalist movement. It is, indeed. And yet many people—Jews and non-Jews, scholars and students among them—point out that Jewish nationalism is set apart from other kinds of nationalism. What do you think? Is Zionism different?

In the space below, list as many ways as you can in which Zionism is special, if you think it is. If you think it is not, tell why.

Chapter 5

THE CHALLENGE OF FREEDOM

FIND THE OUTSIDER*

In each of the statements below, circle the letter before the section that is incorrect.

1. Herz Cerfberr   (a) was like Mendelssohn because his acceptance into Gentile society was a rare exception;   (b) wanted to bring Jews into the mainstream of the industrial economy;   (c) rejected Christian society for its narrow-minded prejudice;   (d) can be compared to a modern ghetto spokesperson who cries out that the people's troubles are not because they do not know how to work, but because society keeps them poor, powerless, and uneducated.

2. For eighteenth and nineteenth century Jews, freedom   (a) was bitterly opposed by many Christians even after laws gave the Jews civil rights;   (b) was a major reason that many renounced their national roots, even converted;   (c) was a challenge that could be positive and creative;   (d) spelled the beginning of the end of centuries of anti-Semitism.

3. The French "Sanhedrin"   (a) improved the situation of French Jews and hastened their acceptance into French society;   (b) pointed up a major difference between Christianity, which is only a religion, and Judaism, which is both a nation and a religion;   (c) demonstrated that French Jews longed to be accepted as full-fledged citizens of France;   (d) brought up the question of Jewish dual loyalty, an issue which has come up many times since.

4. The stories of Christian Dohm, Count Mirabeau, and the country of Holland   (a) show that, at times, anti-Jewish attitudes are the result of misunderstandings and mistaken beliefs rather than hatred and prejudice;   (b) show that nations, and not just people, can be profoundly different from one another;   (c) prove that with wisdom and patience, Jews will one day be fully accepted by all peoples and nations;   (d) remind us that there have been Christians who have supported the Jews as a people.

5. The German anti-Jewish riots of 1819   (a) demonstrated that nationalist feeling could bring about waves of violent anti-Semitism just as religion had been doing for centuries;   (b) were the natural product of the German national character;   (c) came about, in part, as a reaction to Napoleon's actions and ambition;   (d) showed the depth, strength, and intensity of anti-Jewish feelings in Europe.

6. Israel Jacobson   (a) was responsible for discouraging many Jews from converting to Christianity;   (b) showed that Judaism could undergo change and improve, and that freedom need not be an enemy of tradition;   (c) bitterly condemned traditional Judaism as a relic from the Middle Ages;   (d) taught us how greatly important education and communication can be to Jewish life.

INSIGHTS IN DEPTH

Support each of the following statements with a reference to, or a quotation from, the text:

1. Anti-Semitism has a good deal of staying power.

_____

_____

_____

24

2. Nationalism was taking its place alongside religion as a reason to exclude, hate, and persecute the Jews.

_____

_____

_____

3. Acceptance into Gentile society was by no means the only reason that nineteenth century Jews were turning away from tradition; other reasons lay within Judaism itself.

_____

_____

_____

4. Judaism differs from Christianity not only on questions of belief, but in the way it defines itself, as well.

_____

_____

_____

WORD SCRAMBLE*

Unscramble each of the words below to reveal a negative description of nineteenth century European Jews frequently expressed by nineteenth century Christians.

1. **S L A Y O I L D** =

2. **S U D R I T E S O** =

3. **S P Y H U** =

4. **T R E N D E F I F** =

5. **T H A C E S** =

ISSUE

DUAL LOYALTY

The French Christians challenged the loyalty of France's Jews on the grounds that the Jews were still loyal to Eretz Yisrael. This accusation of "dual loyalty" has been made against the Jews from time to time for the past two centuries. In fact, most Jews *do* have a special relationship to the State of Israel, just as the State of Israel has a special relationship and concern with the world Jewish community.

How would you explain this to a non-Jewish friend who asks—out of curiosity, not antagonism—"What is all this business about a special relationship between your people and Israel? Sure, I'd like to visit the country my ancestors came from some day, but I don't go out and defend that country in rallies or tell my children that they should strengthen their ties to it. Do you, in truth, have two loyalties? Do you think of yourself as a Jew first, an American first, or what?"

Try to explain this Jewish problem in your own words, using the space below.

Chapter 6

THE MAKING OF MODERN JUDAISM

TRUE OR FALSE?* (T) (F)

1. Many German Jews who converted to Christianity did so because they thought it was necessary for "getting ahead" in German society. T F

2. According to strict Jewish tradition, an *agunah* might be forbidden to remarry for the rest of her life.   T   F

3. Nineteenth century Conservative Judaism insisted that questions of belief and ritual observance were strictly matters of individual decision.   T   F

4. The sermon is rooted in ancient Jewish history and tradition.   T   F

5. Rabbi Geiger argued that the laws of the Bible and Talmud were obsolete, irrelevant to nineteenth century Jewish needs, and should, therefore, be discarded.   T   F

6. The main reason why traditionalists bitterly opposed the ideas introduced by Reform Jews was that they feared changing Jewish law would lead to assimilation.   T   F

7. The Reformers believed that Judaism must be an "open book," constantly being written and rewritten.   T   F

8. The Jewish woman enjoyed neither respect nor power until Reform and Conservative Judaism insisted upon radical changes in her status.   T   F

9. The "Science of Judaism," as developed by Leopold Zunz, introduced systematic study of Jewish history and tradition. T F

10. Neo-Orthodoxy was based on the idea that Jews could be full and active members of the modern world, while remaining strictly observant and true to the tradition.   T F

SPEAKERS AND SERMONS*

Nineteenth century Germany witnessed the revival of an ancient Jewish custom, the sermon. Rabbis, Reform and traditional alike, saw the sermon as "a tool for instructing the ignorant and exciting the indifferent."

Below are pieces of six imaginary sermons that might have been spoken by six of the personalities mentioned in the chapter and the special topics. See how many you can identify.

1. "We must not give in to the temptations of modern life. We must not become a nation like all other nations. Our strength lies in being special. We were different from the idol worshippers in ancient times, and we must not assimilate or abandon our tradition today. The truth is, we can be a part of the modern world without giving up the laws that God has given us."

_____

2. "I am not complaining about the ancient rabbis. I am simply saying that their values and lifestyle are outdated today. For example, what difference can it possibly make _when_ you pray, as long as you _do_ pray. As for Hebrew, doesn't it make sense to speak to God in a language that we understand, rather than chanting prayers in a whole bunch of Middle Eastern syllables that make little sense to us now?"

_____

3. "I am not going to make any excuses for what I did. I must express myself. God has given me talents that I must use. Anyway, these are the times in which we live. Every Jew must decide what is most important to him or her."

_____

4. "We cannot accept tradition blindly. Judaism is a blend of moral law and ritual observance. The moral law is eternal and unchanging. Rituals are our own invention: they must be examined, improved, sometimes discarded. And every individual must decide which rituals he or she will observe."

_____

5. "We have to avoid the extremes. The need for change is written into the character of Judaism. The Talmud interprets and examines biblical law. The codebooks of the Middle Ages interpret and examine the Talmud. We are a religion on the move. On the other hand, to move too quickly, to discard traditions at random, is like throwing out the baby with the bath water. Allowing each Jew to make decisions about what to observe and how to observe it, is an invitation to chaos and confusion. We are a nation, and our basic unit is the *kehillah*, the community. Let us make our decisions about tradition and change on that basis."

_____

6. "My approach is not as cold as it may sound. What must guide us as Jews is the process of discovery—study, research, thought, and interpretation. And what we are discovering is the meaning of our heritage—the principles and values of Judaism, and how they began."

_____

INTERPRETATION

THE SPIRIT OF THE LAW

Many nineteenth century German Jewish leaders tried to reach beneath the surface of Jewish laws to find the spirit behind them. Reformers did this in order to change or discard certain traditions. The Neo-Orthodox did it to affirm traditions and talk of them in modern ways.

On the next page is a "cycle" of Jewish life, containing customs and traditions we have practiced for centuries. In the

space beside each custom, write in a major idea or value that
you think it expresses—the spirit of the law.

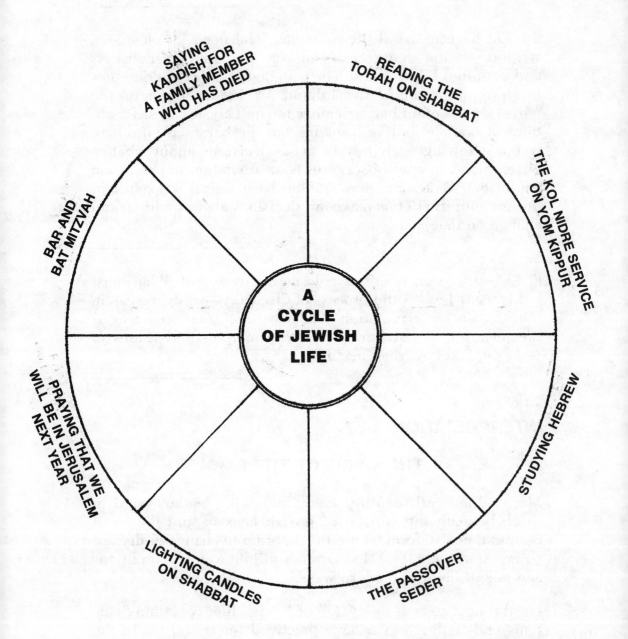

Chapter 7

HEROES OF EMANCIPATION

ACHIEVEMENTS AND AWARDS*

Each of the imaginary awards below describes the achievements of one of the remarkable characters described in this chapter. In the space after the word "To," write in the name of the person being honored.

1. To _____
The distinguished son of a distinguished father, who placed principle and pride of identity over political opportunity again and again; and in so doing, opened the doors of political opportunity to all the Jews of his country.

2. To _____
A true professor in the fine art of self-defense, who put a real monkey wrench in the idea that Jews are physically inferior and unable to take care of themselves.

3. To _____
A man of countless talents and achievements whose greatest gift to his fellow Jews in Palestine was helping them to help themselves.

4. To _____
The leader of Europe's first family of finance, who proved himself a miracle worker in the field of transportation as well—to the everlasting sorrow of that little man who dreamed of being emperor of all Europe.

5. To _____
A lawyer, writer, editor, judge, and statesman who refused to

purchase that well-known ticket of admission to German society, and devoted his life to fighting for equal rights for his people, and all peoples.

6. To _____
Who fought for freedom from poverty, insecurity, financial exploitation, and for the principle that workers must control the means of production, and own what they produced.

7. To _____
A courageous defender of human rights in his native land and abroad who worked tirelessly to abolish the hated "Jewish oath," and who fought without compromise against the obscene Syrian Blood Libels.

LOOKING FOR UNDERSTANDING

Answer the following briefly and clearly.

1. In what way was Sir Moses Montefiore's contribution to the Jewish community of Eretz Yisrael different from contributions of other Jews, rich and poor, who gave tzedakah to the

Holy Land? _____

_____

_____

2. Why have Daniel Mendoza's athletic achievements been considered an important psychological breakthrough for

British Jewry? _____

_____

_____

3. What insight led to the founding of the Alliance Israelite Universelle, and what has the Alliance done during the past

century? _____

_____

_____

4. How did the officers of the Pope justify their kidnapping of a Jewish boy from his home, and what do the results of this case tell us about Jewish life in Europe in the mid-nineteenth

century? _____

_____

_____

5. Why did so many Jews (Riesser, Lassalle, Crémieux, Montefiore, Lionel de Rothschild) involve themselves in the struggle for social, political, economic, and human rights?

_____

_____

_____

6. What were the main reasons that Montefiore and Crémieux were successful in their fight against the Blood Libel charges

in the Damascus Affair? _____

_____

_____

HUNTING HIDDEN WORDS

AN OCCUPATION SCAN*

In the block of letters that follow, seven occupations of people discussed in this chapter are hidden. One of the occupations is written out as two words. The words you are looking for may be written vertically, horizontally, start at the beginning of a line or in the middle, or may turn a corner. Two words may intersect and share a letter. As long as the letters are in consecutive order, they are fine. Circle the seven occupations as you find them.

P	H	I	L	A	N	T	H	R	O
L	O	X	B	A	N	K	E	R	P
A	K	L	M	Q	W	G	Z	X	I
B	V	H	I	W	V	Y	T	N	S
O	F	A	B	T	M	A	E	I	T
R	B	G	E	D	I	T	O	R	X
O	V	O	R	Y	D	C	N	B	Q
R	M	E	X	A	B	W	I	T	W
G	Q	U	R	E	N	A	Z	A	B
A	N	I	Z	E	R	B	R	F	N

A MEDIA MIX*

Imagine how the people and events of the mid-nineteenth century might be treated in today's media—news headlines, editorials, television, radio, and so on. Here are a few imaginary examples. Try to figure out which person or event from the chapter is being described, and write your answer on the line after each media quotation.

1. Headline
   JEWISH IMAGE ROCKED BY RESOUNDING UPPERCUT!
   England Agog!

   _____

2. Editorial
   Call this a nasty coincidence if you like, but this so-called labor organizer who is challenging our free enterprise system, who is plotting against our way of life, and who would make Germany a socialist state, also happens to be a Jew!

   _____

34

3. News Commentary
This is a banner day for all of us. The principle of unity has been defended. From this day on, in the eyes of the law, there are no Jews, and no Christians. We are all French.

_____

4. Headline
**POL WHO DECLARES
"I GOTTA BE ME"
PEAKS AT POLLS FOR
SEVENTH TIME!**
*Wins His Point and
Is Sworn Into Parliament!*

_____

5. Cover of a News Magazine

**Right Versus Right:
Family or Faith?**

_____

6. Television Talk Show
The host: *I agree. It's a primitive country and a backward government. But this is not the first time such an accusation has been made. Are all of these stories really lies? I find that hard to believe. And so must the viewing audience, even though we know that the whole thing is an infamous falsehood.*

_____

THEN AND TODAY

A BRIEF QUESTIONNAIRE

One reason for the study of history is to help us develop attitudes about the people and events of our past. Here's a chance to take your Jewish pulse. Using the questions below, share some of your reactions to this chapter with the other students in your class.

1. Which Jew described in the chapter do you admire the most, and why?

2. Have you ever been exposed to an anti-Semitic idea or image like the Blood Libel, and if so, what was it?

3. Which event in this chapter fills you with the most pride, and why?

4. If you could have changed one thing in the history told in this chapter, what change would you have made?

Chapter 8

AMERICA BEFORE 1880

WHO, OR WHAT, AM I?*

1. I am the rabbi who helped found the first Hebrew Sunday school in the United States. I was also the first to give sermons in the English language in an American synagogue. My name is _____.

2. I am the pioneer and leading organizer of Reform Judaism in the United States during the nineteenth century. I am _____.

3. I am the independent agency founded by Rebecca Gratz, recognized as the parent of today's network of Jewish charitable organizations. I was called _____.

4. I am the occupation shared by many nineteenth century German Jewish immigrants, a few of whom went on to form retailing empires and department store dynasties. The kind of work I am is _____.

5. I am the founder of the largest department store in the United States, but my greatest satisfaction came from promoting the cause of milk pasteurization thus possibly saving the lives of thousands of children. My name is

_____.

6. I am proud to have been able to contribute not only to the various congregations in the United States, but to the Jewish community in Eretz Yisrael as well. I am

_____.

FIND THE OUTSIDER*

Each statement below contains one section that is an "outsider" because it is false. Circle the letter of the false section.

1. Rebecca Gratz (a) was deeply committed to the value of tzedakah; (b) never came into social contact with non-Jews; (c) had the ability to put her ideas into practice; (d) was willing, even eager, to experiment with new approaches when old ways would not work.

2. The photographs and captions on pages 71, 73, 74, 76, and 77 show that (a) American Jews, like the Jews of Russia and Poland, were set apart from the non-Jewish people of their country in dress and appearance; (b) synagogue design could be an art form in its own right, with a variety of styles; (c) if we could somehow travel back through time to the 1880s for occasional shopping trips, we would find amazing bargains; (d) Jewish peddlers and merchants were willing to go "where the action was" to sell their goods.

3. Judah Touro (a) was willing to strike out for parts unknown and live as a stranger; (b) showed his devotion to the United States in a number of different ways; (d) was committed to Jewish communal life in the United States; (d) felt no sense of kinship with the Jewish community in Eretz Yisrael.

4. The German-Jewish immigrants to this country (a) left their native land because they felt oppressed politically, economically, and socially; (b) formed the backbone of the Reform movement in America; (c) kept strictly to themselves, and had as little as possible to do with Jews who did not share their background; (d) quickly and successfully entered the mainstream of Jewish American life.

THE REASONS WHY

Complete the following:

1. The word "Reform" was not used by Isaac Mayer Wise as

he began his organizational work because

2. Jewish learning in the United States was in a sad state in the first half of the nineteenth century because

3. Rebecca Gratz and Rabbi Isaac Leeser founded the first Hebrew Sunday school in the Unites States because

4. Rabbi Wise created a major service on Friday evening because

MAP STUDY

A JEWISH TOUR OF THE UNITED STATES*

The sentences below describe ten places of special interest to Jewish travellers in the nineteenth century. Identify the places

described by putting the appropriate number in the circles on the map.

1. This is the area where the founding father of Gimbel's store began his career as a wandering peddler.

2. Here the first Jewish teacher's training college was created, a college that still exists today.

3. In this city Rabbi Isaac Mayer Wise tried unsuccessfully to introduce major changes in Jewish ritual, ending up with what we might call the "Rosh Hashanah Scandal."

4. Here you will find a beautiful national shrine: the oldest synagogue building in North America, named after that famous philanthropist, Judah Touro.

5. The Gratz family made an important contribution to the American war effort of 1812 in this place.

6. In this city, Rabbi Wise got his "second wind," and Reform Judaism in the United States really took root.

7. It was in this area that the United States began to grow as people moved westward, and among them were the immigrant Jewish peddlers and merchants.

8. Though most people don't realize it, this city was where Judah Touro spent most of his adult years. He may have been one of the first Jewish settlers here, and he did much to build up the Jewish community.

9. This is the city in which the most famous Reform temple in the United States was built; and it also contains the largest number of Jews of any city in the United States, even now.

10. Here, Julius Rosenwald left his father's business and went on to create Sears, Roebuck, and Company—an American institution.

Chapter 9

EASTERN EUROPE BEFORE 1880

AN OVERVIEW*

Use the words in the blocks following the incomplete history below to fill in the blanks.

The early history of the Jews in Eastern Europe is a crazy quilt

of _____. To begin with,
think of how long ago we settled there. They couldn't even

accuse us of being _____; the man had not yet
been born. Then, of course, there were our neighbors, the idol

worshippers, with whom we lived _____.
We should only have been so lucky with their

_____, centuries later.
    The story of the Khazars is truly mind-boggling. The fact is,
they converted to Judaism not because

_____ but because of

_____. Anyway, there we were,
stretched out between the Caspian and Black Seas

_____.
And bigger may not be better, you know, but it certainly can
feel good.
    We did not do too badly when the Russians first came into
power. The Jewish community in Kiev thrived, due in no small

part to _____, a role for
which we were especially suited,

_____.
    With the Mongol invasion, however,

_____. On the one hand, the Mongols were

42

_____11_____; on the other hand, our peace and quiet was bought at the expense _____12_____.

All of this gave rise to a string of dictators, one crueler than the other. "Peter the Great" was one of the noble exceptions to the rule that _____13_____. "Ivan the Terrible" could be called an _____14_____, though his actions put him _____15_____. He achieved _____16_____ murdering Jews _____17_____. Finally, the Cossack's massacres of 1648 taught us _____18_____ and foreshadowed many periods of _____19_____ for the Jews of Eastern Europe. It also demonstrated _____20_____ on a scale that would only be surpassed by _____21_____, some three centuries later.

Still, for all of the _____22_____, Eastern European Jewry managed to produce _____23_____ in terms of scholarship, creativity, and devotion to the traditions of Judaism.

DIARIES AND DATES*

Imagine that you have found a storehouse of diaries of Eastern European Jews. Some are as old as 2,000 years, others were written as late as the eighteenth century. Here are entries from six of the diaries. Your task is to give each of them an approximate date. To help you, here are the six dates you need:

1797	50 B.C.E.
1380	1530
1720	810

Write the correct date for each diary on the line before the entry.

_____ 1. "His enemies call him 'Ivan the Terrible.' Maybe I'm a part of the minority, but I think of him as 'Ivan the Christian Soldier.' He has restored Russian honor, and doubled the size of our empire."

_____ 2. "We've settled in nicely here. My wife and I like the weather, and our children are making friends with youngsters from the neighboring tribe. I find the pagan rituals of the neighbors very colorful, and we've all been invited to see their Festival of Rain. Yes, of course we are a little homesick. I long to pray in the Temple once more before I die. But if I never see the smirking face of another Roman soldier, it can't be too soon for me!"

_____ 3. "All of this land—ours! We embrace Europe and Asia, and one day we will create a single, united empire. Those remaining Khazars were a strange breed. A stiff-necked people, just like their biblical adopted ancestors. We are well rid of them, believe me!"

_____ 4. "Who would have believed that I could ever have liked a Russian czar? Or prayed for his continued good health and long life? But this czar is different. He is kind, understanding, free of anti-Semitism. Maybe he'll start a trend. And maybe our people has a real future in Russia."

_____ 5. "What a fascinating religion we have adopted. Abraham going to settle in the Promised Land, and later arguing with God over the fate of Sodom. Moses teaching the people the Law in the desert. And the laws—so strict, yet so wise and compassionate, so full of social justice and morality."

_____ 6. "How could this have ever come to pass? The Polish state has. disappeared! A country that is no longer a country. But a people can never stop being a people. And I fear that the ones who will suffer most will be the Jewish people—dispersed and divided now among three governments, with the largest number living where they are most hated."

TRUE OR FALSE?* (T) (F)

1. Not all Russian czars were cruel to the Jews.   T   F

2. The Khazars converted to Judaism because they were not happy being Christians.   T   F

3. The Jews have lived in Eastern Europe for as long as there has been a Russian nation.   T   F

4. Eastern European Jews strongly objected to what was happening to the Jews of Western Europe.   T   F

5. Things grew worse for the Jews of Russia when the Eastern Orthodox church came to power there.   T   F

6. Jews from Lithuania and Galicia slowly became the objects of a body of folk tradition.   T   F

7. The Mongol conquests brought 200 years of peace to Eastern Europe and Asia.   T   F

8. The Mongol invasion also resulted in the destruction of whatever freedom and democracy had existed in Russian society. T   F

THEN AND TODAY

INGREDIENTS OF ANTI-SEMITISM

Anti-Semitism has a terrible way of reappearing in the history of the Jews. Of course, our history has its bright spots, too—the well-being of the Jewish community of Kiev, the story of the Khazars, the fact that Jews were invited to settle in Poland. What this proves is that anti-Semitism is not a natural thing, but is "made" by groups and individuals for their own reasons.

The key to combatting anti-Semitism is knowing why and how it is being used. And since anti-Semitism continues to be a concern for every Jew, the study of history can help us better understand it so that we can fight against it.

List below some of the reasons you believe have caused anti-Semitism in the recent or distant past.

Chapter 10

IN SHTETL AND GHETTO

WHO, OR WHAT, AM I?*

1. I am the Hebrew word used to describe the elementary school in which young Jewish boys studied. I am the _____.

2. I am the Ḥasidic rebbe who publicly cried out to God to protest the suffering of my people. My name is _____.

3. I am the occasion that, in the minds and memories of most Eastern European Jews, gave beauty and dignity and hope to their otherwise dreary existence. I am called _____.

4. I am what the bride's family was expected to give to the couple on the occasion of their marriage. I am the _____.

5. I am the word, taken from the German language, that when roughly translated means a Jewish community within a village or small town. Call me the _____.

6. I am the person whose job it was to make sure that young Jewish boys learned the basics of their tradition. My title comes from the Hebrew word meaning "to study." People called me the _____.

7. I am the author most widely known as chronicler of Jewish life in the shtetl. My penname is a classic Hebrew greeting, even though I wrote mainly in the Yiddish tongue. I am _____.

8. I am one way of studying the Talmud in which students see the Talmud as a set of puzzles. I am _____.

9. I am the branch of Hasidism dedicated, as the initials of my name show, to the quest for wisdom, knowledge, and understanding. My followers call me _____.

10. I am the traditional writings, emphasized by Rabbi Israel Salanter and his followers, which deal with questions of morals and ethics in Jewish life. I am called _____.

FIND THE OUTSIDER*

Each statement below contains one section that does not belong. Find and circle the "outsider" section.

1. During the past two centuries, most European Jews (a) lived lives of poverty marked by potential danger; (b) were similar to their Christian neighbors in culture, language, and education; (c) lived in small, closely knit communities known as *shtetlach*; (d) cherished and preserved Jewish laws and customs.

2. The Sabbath (a) was not strictly observed by most Eastern European Jews; (b) is remembered lovingly by Jews of Eastern European origin as one of the high points of their lives; (c) was a special occasion for shtetl Jews—clearly and dramatically set apart from the workaday week; (d) highlighted the ideas of dignity, beauty, and closeness within the family.

3. In the shtetl, Jewish education (a) was highly valued and pursued; (b) produced generations of Jews who knew and were devoted to Judaism; (c) was one thing that kept Jewish life in Eastern Europe alive and well; (d) was less important than earning a living and overcoming poverty.

4. From Solomon Maimon's tale of how his father once tried to marry him off, we learn that (a) marriage was considered a

serious business—too serious to leave to the bride and groom; (b) love in marriage was thought to be unnecessary; (c) a brilliant scholar was considered the best "catch" as a husband; (d) an important part of the wedding ceremony was the sermon given by the groom to his friends and relatives at the wedding.

5. The Jews of the shtetl community (a) would go to great lengths to support and aid young scholars; (b) were sometimes bitterly divided over approaches to Judaism; (c) rejected the customs and life-styles of the city; (d) worked to help the poor, the sick, the elderly, the orphaned, and the needy.

WORD SCRAMBLE*

Each of the six scrambled words below was a key fact of life in the shtetl and in the ghetto. Unscramble them and write them in the boxes that follow. Then, unscramble the circled letters to find something that strengthened and sustained the Jews of Eastern Europe.

1. **VORPEYT**

2. **ETYPI**

3. **MAILYF**

4. **DYSUT**

5. **GRAEND**

6. **SELNSCOSE**

THEN AND TODAY

DIFFERENCES

There are many differences between Jewish life in the shtetl and Jewish life today. Complete the following statements as clearly as you can, just to see how things have changed:

1. While most modern Jews are part of the social, cultural, and economic life of their country, most East European Jews

2. While shtetl Jews had a clear sense of "who they were, and what God expected of them," many Jews today

3. While most Jews today generally feel safe and secure in their countries, Jews of the shtetl and the ghetto

4. While most Jews today measure their success in terms of wealth and professional achievements, shtetl Jews

Chapter 11

IN THE GRIP OF THE CZARS

TRUE OR FALSE?*   (T) (F)

1. The Russian rulers discriminated against the Jews because they thought of the Jews as disloyal outsiders who could not be trusted. T F

2. Russian history proves that anti-Semitism can exist under two very different kinds of governments. T F

3. Catherine the Great created the Pale of Settlement mainly for political and economic, rather than religious, reasons. T F

4. Isaac Ber Levinsohn waged a constant, bitter, battle against the study of Hebrew, Yiddish, and traditional Judaism. T F

5. The anti-Jewish measures of Czars Alexander I and Nicholas I (including the 30-year draft law) were created to weaken ties between the Jews and Jewish life, and to encourage Jews to convert to Christianity. T F

6. Czar Alexander II proved to be a friend and benefactor to Jews from every walk of life. T F

7. The Eastern European maskilim viewed conversion as the necessary ticket of admission to Russian society. T F

8. The maskilim began writing in Yiddish mainly because it was the only language in which they could reach the majority of the Jews. T F

9. Under czarist rule, Russian Jews were strictly forbidden to settle in large cities.   T   F

10. Moving out of the shtetl and the ghetto posed major questions of identity and problems of self-definition for the Jews of Russia.   T   F

IDEA SCRAMBLE

"OPERATION DESTROY"*

This chapter shows how one Russian government after another has tried to eliminate Judaism, a kind of long term "Operation Destroy." Each of the scrambled word groups below was one strategy of destruction. Unscramble them to reveal what the Jews of Russia have been up against.

1. **TO POVERTY THEM POINT OF TAX THE**

_____

2. **THEIR UP COMMUNITIES BREAK**

_____

3. **CITIZENSHIP DENY OF THEM RIGHTS**

_____

4. **AWAY THEM THEIR CHILDREN FROM TAKE**

_____

5. **PARTICULAR CONFINE TO TERRITORY A THEM**

_____

6. **THEIR DESPISE NEIGHBORS IDENTIFY THEM TO THEIR IMITATE OWN ENCOURAGE AND TO**

_____

EVENTS AND EFFECTS*

Match each of the events in the left column with a particular effect that it had in the right column.

1. The works of Mendele Mocher Sforim

_____ Gave Russian Jewry room to breathe after thirty years of extreme cruelty and oppression, and gave them reason to hope for political rights and social acceptance in the Gentile world.

2. The views of Judah Loeb Gordon

_____ Placed restrictions on the movement and activity of Russian Jewry, and led to the establishment of the Pale of Settlement.

3. The reign of Nicholas I

_____ Reached out and communicated to a mass audience of Russian Jews, writing for them and about them.

4. The Haskalah

_____Brought into being a terrible set of measures that tried to destroy the Jewish family. The most dreadful of these was the 30-year draft law.

5. The reign of Alexander II

_____ Tried to widen the social, cultural, and economic horizons of Russian Jews by narrowing the place of Judaism in their lives.

6. The reign of Catherine the Great

_____ Revived Hebrew as a modern language, capable of secular, as well as religious, expression.

Chapter 12

EUROPE AT ITS HEIGHT

MAP STUDY*

Using the maps on page 115 of the text as your reference, identify the following:

1. The country that, in the early nineteenth century, was governed in part by religious authorities.

_____

2. The largest country responsible for cutting Russia down to size after World War I. _____

3. The only European countries that did not change in size or make-up between 1815 and 1920.

_____

4. The body of water shared by the Austro-Hungarian and Ottoman Empires. _____

5. The Middle Eastern state that can be called the "baby" of the British Mandate, since the mandate was entirely responsible for bringing it into being.

_____

6. The body of water that was shared by the Ottoman Empire and Russia. _____

7. The two lands that combined to make up the state known today as Germany. One of these land's names has become a word that means military pride and values.

_____ and _____

LOOKING FOR UNDERSTANDING

Answer each of the following as briefly and clearly as possible:

1. Why were the European nations able to seize power and control in so much of Africa and Asia? _____

_____

_____

_____

2. Why did European nations wish to have control and power in Africa and Asia? _____

_____

_____

3. What, in your opinion, were the most important results of World War I, and why? _____

_____

_____

_____

4. What were the main reasons for the Russian Revolution?

_____

_____

_____

5. In what ways was the country of Japan like a shtetl?

_____

_____

_____

_____

DIARIES AND DATES*

Here is another imaginary assortment of diaries for you to date. Once again, the clues are lines taken from the diaries themselves. And here are the six dates you will need:

1900	1916
1919	1880
1800	1860

_____ 1. "What our leaders have decreed is truly wise. We have been spared the fate of other nations. Our economy thrives. Our main city has grown large. Our society and culture remains untainted by outside influences."

_____ 2. "Dear God, will it ever end? It seems as though this blood-soaked trench has been my home forever. We are all sacrifices, all lost because of the unbelievable stupidity of our leaders."

_____ 3. "Well, here's to Her Majesty's endless empire. Asia, Africa, and now India! And I've got to hand it to that Jew—he is one smart politician, regardless of his background, and where his grandfather may have gone to pray."

_____ 4. "All things considered, that show of force from the New World has not been such a bad thing for us. We can learn a lesson from them. We will use their science to improve our society and make us strong. Now we have a real army. And a school system."

_____ 5. "This whole business makes me nervous. Twice in two years: major rebellions which we managed to put down just because we had the guns. Doesn't anyone in authority realize that one day these so-called 'backward natives' will get guns, learn to use them, and then where will we be?"

_____ 6. "How does the old saying go? Out of the frying pan and into the fire. Is that all our revolution will be? Just a replacement of one kind of tyranny with another? It's clear that this is not what the people want. They voted against this by a wide margin. Which only goes to prove, that might often makes for power."

HUNTING HIDDEN WORDS*

Hidden in the diagram below are eight political "isms" that have strongly influenced the history of the nineteenth and twentieth centuries. They may be written vertically, horizontally, diagonally, starting at the beginning of a line or in the middle, or may turn around a corner. The words may intersect and share letters. Hunt them down and circle them.

C	O	M	M	U	N	I	S	M	S	P
O	B	Z	D	R	A	M	N	I	O	M
L	Q	I	N	A	T	P	A	L	C	A
O	X	O	B	F	I	E	Z	I	I	H
N	R	N	A	F	O	R	I	T	A	T
I	G	I	R	T	N	I	S	A	L	I
A	Z	S	Q	U	A	A	M	R	I	S
L	W	M	H	C	L	L	K	I	S	K
I	Y	C	E	H	I	I	J	S	M	U
S	F	T	S	O	S	S	F	M	K	F
M	E	L	N	R	M	M	T	O	C	H

Chapter 13

DEATH OF AN OLD DREAM, BIRTH OF A NEW

PERSPECTIVES*

Use the word groups below to complete this short piece of Jewish history.

The assassination of Czar Alexander II destroyed

_____ that Russian Jews had harbored during his reign[1]. His son, Alexander III was an anti-Semite and

needed something _____ from their anger against the government. His[2] plan worked; the Jews

proved to be _____[3].

   A tidal wave of violence was unleashed against Jews all over Russia. A new word came into existence—"pogrom": a riot,

_____
[4]

in which Christians attacked Jewish communities, smashing, looting, murdering. What was most alarming about this was that the so-called "better" parts of society,

_____, looked
[5]
on, and either did nothing, or approved of what was

happening. Of course, the police _____, except
[6]

they sometimes punished Jews _____ against
[7]
the pogromists. Russia might have been divided every which way—rich against poor, peasant against intellectual, czarist against revolutionary—but when it came to attacking Jews,

they _____.
[8]

   The May Laws _____ to methods of
[9]

persecution and discrimination. The Jews were torn from their homes and communities, kept from entering schools and universities, and driven into poverty on a mass scale. And

_____, they could not protest, they could not protect themselves. And the Kishinev pogrom cruelly illustrated
10

_____ violence could erupt, with the Jew again and again cast _____.
11   12
These, and other events, triggered the realization among many

Jews that _____ in Russia. The
13
overwhelming majority _____; however, a
14
small number of Jews became convinced that life in the

Diaspora _____, and so they turned
15

eastward, embraced _____, and dreamed of
16
_____ in Eretz Yisrael.
17

who dared to fight back   lent legal respectability

stripped of their rights as they were

most often organized and set into motion by the government

to divert the Russian people

sat on their hands

convenient scapegoats

students, writers, and members of the middle class

in the role of helpless victim

the hopes and dreams

achieved unity, and worked together in harmony

the Zionist idea

creating a Jewish homeland

there was no real future for them

was at best an "iffy" proposition

how easily and suddenly

came to America

WHO, WHAT, OR WHERE AM I?*

1. I gave huge sums of money to support Jewish settlement in Palestine. My name is _____.

2. Because of me, and what is written in me, the Jews have often been accused of conspiring to destroy Christianity and take over the whole world. My title is

_____.

3. I was there when the Russians accused a Jew of the Blood Libel. My worst problem was, I was the Jew who was accused. My name is _____.

4. I am the word for the organized, violent, anti-Jewish riots that occurred in the reign of Czar Alexander III—and I have been used to speak of events of this sort ever since. I am a

_____.

5. I am the network of laws—devised during the reign of Czar Alexander III—that took away the rights of the Jews, drove many of them from their homes, forced many out of schools and universities, and gave power to their Christian neighbors. Call me _____.

6. In this city vicious riots occurred in which 47 Jews were massacred. The city name is _____.

7. I have been called the greatest modern Hebrew poet. Yet I have lived in what must be one of my people's most evil moments. My name is _____.

8. I am the name, made up of Hebrew initials, given to the first group of Zionist pioneers to settle in Palestine in 1882. They were called the _____.

THEN AND TODAY

TURNING POINTS

The Russian pogroms marked a major turning point in Jewish history. Mass migration to America was speeded up, and the belief in Zionism grew stronger. Recently, a new turning point came in the creation of the State of Israel in 1948. In the space below, write down as many changes in Jewish life as you can think of that came about because of the creation of the Jewish State.

Chapter 14

THE HERZL MIRACLE

*NEGATIVE HEADLINES AND COMMENTS**

Even when something seems popular or positive, there is always someone or some group that sees it as negative. Each of the negative comments, editorials, or headlines below refers to a particular event—some which most of us would say were quite positive. See if you can identify the events from this unusual point of view.

1. **DARK DAY FOR CHRISTIAN PATRIOTS! TRAITOR GOES FREE!**

   _____

2. *"The nicest way to speak of this is as a gathering of dizzy dreamers and not-too-bright thinkers. They have come from all over the world to play 'country' the way little children play 'house.'"*

   _____

3. *"These people defile everything holy. They don't talk, dress, or act like religious Jews. They don't study or pray. They stay away from our centers of Jewish life and behave mostly like non-Jews. "Farmers" they fancy themselves. Since when do Jews work on the land?"*

   _____

4. **LYING JUDAS LEAVES COUNTRY! OUTRAGED CITIZENS STORM STREETS IN PROTEST!**

   _____

5. *"This minor best seller can have fearful consequences for*

Jews the world over. Our enemies will pounce on it as proof of Jewish disloyalty to our countries of origin. It will destroy years of hard work and the efforts of hundreds of Jews to bridge the gap between Jews and Christians."

---

6. *"These Jews are ungrateful, and worse. They said they needed a refuge, and so we gave them a safe place. Now they say that the place must also belong to them. Well, they are more likely to get nothing than something this time!"*

THE REASONS WHY

Complete the following statements in your own words:

1. The supposed crime of one Jew (Dreyfus) inspired French mobs to rampage through the streets—looting, burning, beating up, and crying "Down with the Jews" because

2. Herzl believed that the Jewish people must have a state of their own because

3. Many Jews worried about the creation of a Jewish state in Palestine because

A VALUE SCAN*

Read the Special Topic on page 135. Now look at the seven values listed below. One of them does not belong with the others. Which value is not expressed by the history and idea of the little "Blue Box"?

1. A sense of responsibility for Jews in other lands.
2. Giving tzedakah.
3. Defying unjust authority.
4. A feeling of connection with the Land of Israel.
5. The idea that we must take responsibility for our own defense.
6. Redeeming the soil, and making the desert bloom.
7. Honoring the past and having faith in the future.

INTERPRETATIONS

Read the Special Topic, "Dreyfus in Kasrilevka" (pp. 130–131 in the text), then answer the following:

1. What does Sholem Aleichem's story tell us about the Jews living in the shtetls of Eastern Europe in terms of

    (a) their daily lives? _____

_____

_____

    (b) the way they felt about, and acted toward, the outside world? _____

_____

_____

    (c) the way they felt about Jews in other lands? _____

_____

_____

2. Why did the people react as they did—not against the generals, the judges, or the French, but against Zeidel?

_____

_____

_____

THEN AND TODAY

GUILT BY GENERALIZATION

In his diaries, Theodor Herzl noted that "The Dreyfus case contains . . . the wish of the vast majority in France to damn one Jew and through him all Jews. 'Death to the Jews' the crowd yelled." This is a rather violent example of guilt by generalization. Have you ever heard an entire group blamed for the faults or sins of one of its members? Do you ever find yourself tempted to apply this sort of reasoning? There are many products of guilt by generalization floating around today. What are some of the stereotypes that have been applied to Jews? Blacks? Irish? Italians? Women? Elderly people? Young people? Any other group that you know of, which has been a victim of guilt by generalization?

Chapter 15

THE GOLDEN LAND

FIND THE OUTSIDER*

In each statement below there is one section that does not belong. Find the "outsider" and circle it.

1. The United States (the "Golden Land") (a) was a haven for European immigrants because it offered freedom and opportunity; (b) needed immigration so that there would be enough workers for its fast-growing industries; (c) was attractive to Jews because of its total lack of anti-Semitism; (d) became a major center of Jewish life between 1880 and 1924.

2. Emma Lazarus (a) grew up in a relatively assimilated home; (b) rejected the "uptowners" because of their negative attitudes toward the newcomers; (c) was impressed by the way the "downtowners" stuck to tradition; (d) came to believe that the only answer for the Jewish people was to live in Eretz Yisrael.

3. The Lower East Side (a) was a vital center of Jewish religion during the first decades of this century; (b) contained the largest single group of Eastern European Jewish immigrants to this country; (c) was, in many ways, like a large shtetl transplanted from the Old Country; (d) was the only place that penniless, poorly paid Jews could afford to live in New York.

4. The Jewish immigrant worker (a) found employment, for the most part, in big-city industries; (b) was forced to work oppressively long hours for pitifully small wages; (c) was usually faced with the choice of working on the Sabbath, or not

working at all;   (d) was soon involved with the struggle to create labor unions and other means of securing workers' rights.

5. Yiddish   (a) was the language spoken by the overwhelming majority of Eastern European Jewish immigrants;   (b) was a source of embarrassment to the uptown Jews;   (c) gave rise to a theatrical tradition that—in addition to becoming an institution in American life—served as an outlet of relief, escape, and entertainment for the hard-pressed newcomers;   (d) was the source of a rich and varied culture that gave a sense of unity to the downtown Jews.

HUNTING HIDDEN WORDS*

In the block of letters below are eight words that were a part of the American Jewish "downtown" experience at the turn of the century. They may be written vertically, horizontally, diagonally, starting at the beginning of a line or in the middle, or may be found turning a corner. Two words (or even three) may intersect and share a letter. As long as the letters of the word are in some kind of consecutive order, they are fine. Hunt down the eight words, and circle them.

A	N	E	W	S	P	A	P	E	R
C	M	F	P	N	K	N	T	U	E
Q	U	L	K	F	Z	X	F	Z	D
T	P	S	A	S	H	U	L	G	U
R	H	W	X	B	E	N	F	Q	C
Y	J	E	F	A	M	I	L	Y	A
I	W	A	A	Y	E	O	I	H	T
D	O	T	H	T	D	N	P	N	I
D	Y	S	M	G	E	L	U	J	O
I	S	H	O	P	B	R	M	L	N

TESTIMONIALS*

At testimonial dinners we give praise to people who have achieved something special with their lives. There are many such people discussed in this chapter. Imagine yourself at a few testimonial dinners, and try to guess from these bits taken from the speeches who is being honored in each case.

1. "He gave up the quiet and security of being a scholar to enter the frantic, uncertain world of the American Jewish community—just when we needed him most."

_____

2. "His was not a vision of cities and factories. He dreamt of Jewish farmers—and, maybe, Jewish cowboys—and his dreams were a little like those of the Zionist pioneers. An uncommon man. A uniquely generous person."

_____

3. "As Sholom Aleichem expresses the soul and spirit of Eastern Europe's Jews, so this person expresses its conscience. Every man, woman, and child who has to work 16 hours a day in the sweatshops has good reason to thank him, to bless him for helping to make his or her life bearable, and for providing hope."

_____

4. "Among her many gifts, which have meant so much to her fellow Jews, those that come most warmly to mind are 'teacher,' 'learner,' 'humanitarian,' and 'visionary.'"

_____

5. "How does one measure the gift of pleasure—the stories, the music, the laughter, the memories—that he has given to the poor, struggling Jews? Many others came after him, but he was the first. A true folk-artist. A performer of the people."

_____

THEN AND TODAY

GENERATION GAPS

As the Jews adjusted to new ways of life in America, children and parents seemed to grow further apart. The children could adapt more easily; it took the parents far longer, and many never really adapted to life in the Golden Land.

There are always distances between generations, ways in which children differ in their ideas and values and attitudes from their parents. There may be great differences, as there were 70 or 80 years ago, or the differences may be small.

To get some idea of the differences, the "gap," between your generation and the generation of your parents, fill out the chart below. Tell how you feel about the things listed on the left, and how you think your parents feel about them.

	YOU	YOUR PARENTS
1. Jewish Education		
2. The need to learn Hebrew or Yiddish		
3. Sabbath observance		
4. Tzedakah		
5. The State of Israel		

Chapter 16

NEW LEADERS, NEW OPPORTUNITIES

A MEDIA MIX*

To which events in this chapter do each of the following media descriptions refer?

1. Editorial

"And while we sympathize, and admire, the concerns of these distinguished gentlemen for the well-being of their coreligionists in more oppressive countries (particularly in light of the Kishinev outrages a few years ago), we question the wisdom of creating an international protection agency. Surely, Jews here can count on the government to protect them; and Jews in other countries should do the same."

_____

2. Live Coverage

"Ladies and gentlemen, this may indeed be a great moment in history–even though it is taking place in rather ordinary surroundings. Most of the people around seem rather average, most in their mid-twenties. The land here looks like no one has tended it for centuries. And all these people have bought is a few tents, cots, pots and pans, and some old-fashioned tools. Most of them come from city life. They look as if they don't know what to do here. But every one of them I have spoken to insists that he or she is here to stay. Keep tuned to this station, and we will let you know how this experiment in living turns out. And now, back to you, Harry."

_____

3. Interview

Question: *"Let me understand you, sir. All that money? To a foreign government? So that they can wage war? Why?"*
Answer: *"Perhaps the best way of explaining is with an old saying, 'My enemy's enemy is my friend!'"*

_____

4. News commentary

"This is a proud moment in our history. Jewish people are united; they seem to be saying: 'All of Israel is bound to one another.' Perhaps it is true that two Jews usually have three opinions, but many Jews will band together for the common good of all world Jewry in a time of need or crisis."

5. Headline

CONGRESS CHOOSES PRINCIPLE OVER PRACTICALITY!
Declares *"No Double Standard, Now or Ever!"*

6. News Story

In Jewish tradition, Ḥanukkah is the story of a miracle. And it celebrates the liberation of the Jewish nation from foreign rule. Well, this twentieth century event bears witness to the fact that miracles still can happen. The City of David has been liberated from foreign rule. And these soldiers—they seem like modern Maccabees!"

7. Television Talk Show

Host: *"I think that this move, made with the best of intentions, makes the Jews more vulnerable than they have been in a long time. Aren't you afraid that the enemies of the Jewish people will take advantage of this moment?"*

Guest: *"I think that you are overreacting. Things are not nearly as bad as they seem. There is a vast difference between a "home" and a "state." We have to make this clear, to our own people and to the world."*

WHO, WHAT, OR WHERE AM I?*

1. I was the chairman of the War Industries Board. My job was to convert peacetime industries to making what was needed for the war effort as quickly and efficiently as possible. My name is ―――――――――.

2. I am proud to be a Jew, proud to be a cabinet member, and proud to support the Zionist cause. I am ―――――――――.

3. I was David Ben Gurion's first home away from home. I am a small, flourishing city in Israel today. My name, translated from Hebrew, means "The Opening (or Beginning) of Hope." But you call me _____.

4. I have been called a Wall Street wheeler-dealer. Maybe I am. But I also believe in wheeling and dealing for my people. That's why I helped to found the American Jewish Committee. My name is _____.

5. I am another kind of settlement in Israel, and I try to combine the best of both worlds. My members are mainly farmers. They market their goods collectively, but live and work on their own farms. Folks call me a _____.

WORD SCRAMBLE*

Each of the scrambled words below is an important part of life on the kevutzah and kibbutz. Unscramble the words. Then, unscramble the circled letters to reveal a vision that gave hope to the pioneers of the Second Aliyah.

1. **G R A F I M N**

2. **D R E M O F E**

3. **L A I Q U Y T E**

4. **G R I S H A N**

5. **G R I E P E N I O N**

Chapter 17

DEPRESSION AND WORLD CONFLICT

DIARIES AND DATES*

You've done it again! You've found six more diaries of the imagination. Try to guess from the entries below the correct dates of each diary. The dates you need this time are:

1920	1932
1938	1940
1946	1935

_____ 1. "In two short years, that man we once called a buffoon and a fanatic has become the absolute ruler of his country. His will has become the law of the land. And people there are marching and singing and obeying him blindly."

_____ 2. "That poor simple guy. Did he really believe all those noble things he spoke about? Peace on earth forever? Total disarmament? An international community? Justice and mercy toward the fallen enemy? In the end, of course, the politicians of Europe taught him a lesson: To the victor belong the spoils!"

_____ 3. "Chamberlain is being hailed as a hero now, for having brought about 'Peace in our time.' But all he has really done is to purchase a few months of relief from Hitler's threats and tirades. And what is likely to be the price of this momentary silence? Czechoslovakia!"

_____ 4. "Well, the nightmare is finally over. More than 40 million people have been killed. The near destruction of

European Jewry. Hitler is dead, and Germany has gone down to defeat. The question is, what have we learned from all this? Will we create a safer, saner world order, or will we continue to stumble along blindly from chaos and tragedy to destruction and holocaust?"

_____ 5. "Everything too little and too late. Now that war has finally been declared, Hitler has overrun almost all of Europe. And he has signed a treaty with Russia. He seems absolutely unbeatable. Democracy in Europe is now dead. What will become of us? The future looks so dim and hopeless. And, so terrifying."

_____ 6. "It's incredible! Two years ago, I would never have imagined such a thing. But the impossible suddenly seems real. This funny-looking little man is promising people a better and more glorious tomorrow; and the people, sick of bread lines and unemployment, are really listening to him!"

LOOKING FOR UNDERSTANDING

Answer each of the following questions as clearly and briefly as you can:

1. How did the harsh conditions placed on Germany after World War I help pave the way for Hitler? _____

_____

_____

2. Why does a period of runaway inflation become a good time to overthrow a government (as it was for Hitler)? _____

_____

_____

3. How did the policy of appeasement practiced by France and England in the hope of avoiding war, actually help to bring on the war? _____

_____

_____

TRUE OR FALSE?*   (T) (F)

1. France and England gave in to Hitler's demands again and again because the German military machine was simply too powerful to defy.   T   F

2. The Great Depression played a large role in bringing Hitler to popularity and power.   T   F

3. The United States did not enter World War II until more than two years after it began.   T   F

4. The actions of the German Communists gave Hitler an excuse to destroy all non-Nazi parties and to become the absolute dictator of Germany.   T   F

5. One of Hitler's goals, apart from his war aims, was the slaughter of the entire Jewish people.   T   F

LESSONS OF HISTORY

What lesson can you learn from each of the following events or developments? (There may be many lessons to learn, but just list one for each.)

Lesson

1. The behavior of the Allies toward Germany after World War I
_____
_____
_____

2. Hitler's rise to power
_____
_____
_____

3. Hitler's 'peaceful' conquests (for example, Austria and Czechoslovakia) in the years before World War II
_____
_____
_____
_____

4. The staggering loss of
human lives in World
War II

    _____

    _____

    _____

THEN AND TODAY

DANGER SIGNALS

Before a Hitler can arise, or a society can go mad, there are danger signals. Looking back, we can see the danger signals in Germany pretty clearly. People were hungry, out of work, poor, discouraged, and tired of weak leaders.

It's more difficult when we try to see the danger signals in our own times. Are there any problems you can think of in today's society that might lead us in the wrong directions? In the column on the left below, list two or three of today's danger signals. In the column on the right, make a suggestion for what we might do about these problems to keep them from getting out of hand.

DANGER SIGNALS	SUGGESTIONS FOR IMPROVEMENTS

Chapter 18

PRELUDE TO DISASTER

LOGICAL LESSONS*

Anti-Semitism is an example of the lack of logic at work. Yet, prejudice continues to be a problem, even in modern times. Under each of the historical developments below are three lessons that we might learn from it. Only one of them can be logically drawn from that development. Circle the letter beside the lesson you think is the logical one.

1. The Leo Frank case shows that
   (a) Jews should have known better than to have settled in the deep South;
   (b) anti-Semitism can take a turn for the violent, even in a democracy;
   (c) when a child is murdered, people will go to almost any lengths to punish the murderer.

2. The history of restrictions and quotas against Jews in the United States teaches that
   (a) Europe, where many Jews were able to become doctors and lawyers, was far less anti-Semitic than the United States;
   (b) there was an attempt to keep Eastern European Jewish immigrants out of high-paying professions;
   (c) anti-Semitism can often become the law of the land.

3. The life stories of Henry Ford and Charles A. Lindbergh show that
   (a) anti-Semitism was widespread among American celebrities in the 1920s and 1930s;
   (b) people who work with machines are likely to be more prejudiced than writers, teachers, and musicians;
   (c) someone may be both a person of great accomplishments *and* an anti-Semite.

4. The Johnson Act teaches that

(a) a simple law can affect the lives of millions of people, even change the course of history;

(b) Hatred and prejudice can often dictate a country's policies;

(c) the American people in general, and Congress in particular, disliked the inpouring of foreigners after World War I.

5. The work of Louis Marshall shows that

(a) in order to be a successful defender of Jewish rights, a person must be committed to the rights of all minorities;

(b) the forces of prejudice and discrimination in this country between the World Wars could be fought and sometimes defeated;

(c) German Jews have led the struggle for human rights in the United States.

INDIVIDUALS AND THEIR IDEAS*

To which individual discussed in the chapter does each of the following ideas belong?

1. "We must stop 'thinking narrow.' We must define Judaism in social terms. In cultural terms. In communal terms. In terms of peoplehood and nationality. I don't say that the religious part is not important; just that it is not everything."

_____

2. "The thing is, we 'moderns' have lost our religious vocabulary. We have forgotten how to talk about God, and how to talk to God. But remember, we are the losers when we frighten ourselves by thinking of God as too complex to understand."

_____

3. "I don't agree that we should stay quiet so that the Gentiles won't think of us as 'pushy.' No, sir. Prejudice won't vanish by itself. What we are looking at here is a question of right and wrong. Restrictions are wrong. Quotas are wrong. We must fight these things publicly, as matters of the deepest principle!"

_____

4. "Their concern for their fellow Jews is understandable. But can we allow the interests of one minority group, Jewish or otherwise, to push this country into war against a nation with which we have no real quarrel? I do not believe the American people would want to go to war for the sake of the Jews."

_____

5. "I guess you could say that my approach is summed up by the word 'relevance.' I want Jewish tradition to relate to our daily lives, here and now. There is a connection, and that's for sure. Judaism is meant to be used, not just observed. Just as Hebrew has become a living language, so Judaism must be a living tradition."

_____

IDEA SCRAMBLE*

Unscramble the word groups in the circles below to find a variety of ideas about the Jewish people. Some of these ideas come from Jews. Others come from Gentiles. Some are the ideas of the anti-Semites discussed in this chapter.

1. OVER PLOTTING
WORLD IS INTERNA-
TIONAL TO JEWRY
TAKE THE

_____
_____
_____
_____

2. COMPLETE IS WAY
JUDAISM A LIFE OF

_____
_____

3. WITH A COMMUNI-
CATE ON PERSONAL
GOD JEWS BASIS MUST

_____
_____
_____

4. BE A TRADITIONAL
EXAMINED PROBLEMS
VIEWPOINT MODERN
CAN FROM

_____
_____
_____
_____

5. AGAINST MUST OF
JEWS ANY RESTRIC-
TIONS FIGHT KIND

_____

_____

_____

THEN AND TODAY

AN ACTIVITY HUNT

One of Mordecai Kaplan's teachings was that Judaism is a complete way of life, and that the Jewish community can serve a variety of purposes. Study the program calendar of your own synagogue, or think about what activities go on in your synagogue or community center, and see if you can list:

1. An activity that makes us proud of being Jewish.

_____

2. An activity that helps to strengthen the family.

_____

3. An activity that creates a sense of closeness with Israel.

_____

4. An activity that deepens our feeling for, and attachment to, Jewish tradition.

_____

5. An activity that makes us aware of, and sensitive to, Jewish suffering or tragedy.

_____

Chapter 19

THE HOLOCAUST

A REVIEW

This chapter of the text tells of things that defy the imagination. It is difficult to make comparisons or to interpret the events of these terrible years. Perhaps the best that can be done is to ensure that we have the facts straight, and then to ask a few basic questions—questions that may not have hard and fast answers.

* * * *

IDENTIFY*

1. The group of laws that stripped German Jews of their citizenship and their legal rights.

_____

2. The name by which the Nazis described their "race."

_____

3. The Nazi phrase which sounded harmless at first, but which was really a code meaning the destruction of the Jews.

_____

4. Hitler's Minister of Propaganda who stirred up the German people against the Jews and prepared the Germans for "acts which no moral human being would perform."

_____

5. The method the Nazis used for cleansing the German mind of Jewish ideas (and some non-Jewish ideas, as well).

_____

6. The event—including the smashing of Jewish homes, the looting and burning of Jewish businesses, and the arrest of tens of thousands of Jews—that marked the end of organized Jewish life in Germany.

_____

7. Another people, aside from the Jews, marked for total extermination by the Germans.

_____

8. The concentration camp in which Anne Frank met her death.

_____

9. The concentration camp in which the largest number of Jews were murdered.

_____

10. The monument set up in Jerusalem in honor of the Jews murdered during the Holocaust.

_____

GENERAL QUESTIONS

1. What methods did the Nazis use to prepare the German people to take part in the Holocaust? _____

_____

_____

2. Why did the Nazis burn the books of great writers and thinkers, Jewish and non-Jewish? _____

_____

_____

3. Hitler set forth his racist views and his military goals for conquest quite openly. Why, then, did so many Germans vote

him into office? _____

_____

_____

4. The kind of public humiliation shown in the photograph on page 169 of the text was not uncommon. In fact, such photos were taken by the Nazis as "souvenirs," of which they were proud. But it served no military or economic purpose; it was just aimless cruelty. What, in your opinion, did the Nazis have in mind? _____

_____

_____

5. The businessman who produced the cremation ovens may well have been a good citizen, a devoted son, a loving husband and father, a regular churchgoer, a good neighbor. How could he write such a letter (p. 173)? _____

_____

_____

PHOTO EVIDENCE*

Modern historians study photographs very carefully—for what they say, and for what they don't say. Below are eight statements that might be made after studying the photographs and illustrations in this chapter (pp. 169, 170, 171, 172, 173, 177). One of them is in no way taken from the photographs or illustrations. Circle the number before the one that does not belong here.

1. During their early years in power, the Nazis took steps to cripple the German Jews economically.

2. The Nazis performed acts of pointless personal cruelty against Jews.

3. Thousands of Jews died in forced labor camps, as well as in death camps.

4. In their early persecution of Jews, the Nazis did not hesitate to include children and the elderly.

5. Jewish slave laborers lived in horrible conditions.

6. The State of Israel has gone to great lengths to honor the memory of the Holocaust victims.

7. The Germans were especially cruel to Orthodox Jews.

8. The Germans murdered the Jews in masses, in an assembly-line fashion.

DIARIES AND DATES*

Continue the work of a historian by trying to date the entries taken from these six imaginary diaries. The dates you will need are not tied to an exact event—they are approximate.

1940	1938
1932	1944
1936	1943

_____ 1. "The mass murders go on at an incredible rate. Only a few months ago hundreds of thousands of Hungarian Jews went through this camp. Now they are no more."

_____ 2. "Our cousins in America are celebrating Thanksgiving. But what do we have to be thankful for? Our home is a shambles; our business has been looted. Father was arrested in the middle of the night. We should have left Germany years ago. Now, with this fine that they want us to pay, there is no money for tickets—let alone for a bribe to get past the border. And, is there any country that would take us in?"

_____ 3. "I have spoken to three people today, and all of them are voting for the Nazis. Hitler, they tell me, will restore order and bring an end to the unemployment. One said that I should stop worrying about Hitler's anti-Semitism. All that will end once Hitler is in power, he said."

_____ 4. "How can I describe it? Huge numbers of Jews are being moved eastward. Ghettos are springing up all over Eastern Europe; and Jews are being jammed into them at a staggering rate. And there are stories, tales of horrors, being whispered all around."

_____ 5. "The ghettos are being emptied out. The Nazis say that the Jews are being sent to the East, to work. But some people in the ghetto, especially the young people and the Zionists, tell us not to believe a word the Germans say. Can it be that the Germans are really sending these people—men, women, and children—to their deaths?"

YOUR OWN FEELINGS

INTERPRETATIONS

On pages 173 and 176 are poems and writings of children who were sent to the camp at Terezin. Read and consider them, then write your own feelings about what was happening to these children. If you like, you can express yourself in poetry; if not, just write out your reaction in your own words.

Chapter 20

RESISTANCE TO HITLER

TRUE OR FALSE?* (T) (F)

1. The French government which came to power after the Nazi occupation cooperated with the Germans in rounding up French Jews to be sent to their deaths.   T   F

2. The country of Denmark was the only European Christian country to help the Jews.   T   F

3. The Warsaw Ghetto uprising lasted as long as it did because there were crack combat units among the Jewish freedom fighters.   T   F

4. The Warsaw Ghetto uprising was a source of embarrassment to the Germans.   T   F

5. The Nazis did not kill Leo Baeck because he was known and respected throughout the world.   T   F

6. There were boatloads of Jews forced to return to Europe because they could find no country that would accept them.   T   F

7. Anne Frank's belief "that people are really good at heart" was based mainly on her innocence. Locked up in her small hiding place, she really had no idea of how cruel and destructive the Germans were.   T   F

8. Resistance to the Nazis took many different forms.   T   F

INSIGHTS IN DEPTH

Support each of the following general statements with a specific reference to, or quotation from, the text:

1. Some major world leaders seemed to be accepting Jewish suffering without too much concern. _____

_____

_____

_____

2. The governments and peoples of Nazi-occupied Europe had many differing attitudes toward the Jews—from anti-Semitic beliefs which led them to cooperate with the Nazis, to empathy which led them to protect their Jewish neighbors.

_____

_____

_____

3. The Germans planned carefully the mass murder of the Jews and carried it out according to their plans.

_____

_____

_____

4. Jews often resisted even against impossible odds.

_____

_____

_____

THE RESISTANCE*

Every act of resistance discussed in this chapter had its effects. The statements below speak of these effects, but in each statement there is one section that does not belong. Circle the section that is not an effect.

1. The Warsaw Ghetto uprising
   (a) shocked and embarrassed the German authorities;
   (b) proved that there were many Jews who were willing to die fighting rather than give in to the Nazis;
   (c) inspired the Polish Christians to lay aside their prejudices and join the Jews in fighting the Nazis.

2. The American Jewish Joint Distribution Committee
   (a) made the American public aware of the sad plight of the Jewish refugees;
   (b) set up an underground network of communications and aid that reached into the concentration camps;
   (c) saved the lives of thousands of Jews by smuggling them out of Nazi-occupied Europe.

3. The efforts of the Danish people
   (a) allowed the Danish Jews to live with little fear or hardship during the first years that the Nazis occupied Denmark;
   (b) forced the Germans to act more secretly and cover their tracks better, for fear that this kind of resistance might spread;
   (c) saved practically all Danish Jewry from Nazi slaughter.

4. Youth Aliyah
   (a) helped save the lives of some 30,000 Jewish children;
   (b) helped the rescued children to build new lives in Eretz Yisrael;
   (c) embarrassed the American government by proving that works of rescue and refuge could easily be carried out.

5. The spiritual resistance of Jews in Poland
   (a) created a sense of unity and purpose within the ghettos;
   (b) was a constant source of frustration to the Nazis who wished to stamp out religious activities;
   (c) proved that a way of life with its heritage and traditions could be a source of strength in the most difficult of times.

INDIVIDUALS AND THEIR ACHIEVEMENTS*

Match the individual in the left column with the achievement, or achievements, in the right column. (You may use a number more than once, since some of these individuals had many accomplishments mentioned in the chapter.)

1. Henrietta Szold

_____ Led the Warsaw Ghetto uprising.

2. Anne Frank

_____ A leader and spokesperson for German Jewry who refused to leave the Jewish community in its time of need.

3. King Christian

_____ Founder of Hadassah, the Women's Zionist Organization of America.

4. Rabbi Leo Baeck

_____ Wrote a diary which is still thought to be a celebration of the human spirit in impossible times and difficult circumstances.

5. Mordecai Anilewicz

_____ Defied the Germans, rejecting their demands to isolate the Jewish population for deportation—and inspired a nation to do the same.

_____ Founded Youth Aliyah, helping to save the lives of some 30,000 children.

_____ Inspired and consoled Jews in the concentration camps. Through work, courage, and faith, this person's life came to stand for the real meaning of spiritual resistance.

Chapter 21

THE JEWISH STATE REBORN

WHO, OR WHAT, AM I?*

1. I am the Arab leader who came to an agreement with Dr. Weizmann as to how lands in the Middle East could be divided between our peoples. My name is _____.

2. I am a Jew and a Zionist. Sadly, while I was British high commissioner in Palestine I had to watch, helpless, as my government moved further and further away from creating a Jewish state. I am _____.

3. As Arab violence in Eretz Yisrael grew, the Jews of the Yishuv created me. I am the policy called _____.

4. I am the state, created by the British government out of fully 3/4 of the land of Palestine, and turned over to an Arab government. I am _____.

5. I am the name given to the Arab violence that brought about the slaughter of 133 Jews. I am called _____.

6. Along with Great Britain, I was a country that helped to poison the relationship between Jews and Arabs. I just wanted colonies, pure and simple. My name is _____.

7. I am the name of the document written in 1939 that stopped the large flow of Jewish immigrants to Palestine. I am called the _____.

8. As a force of Jewish soldiers fighting with the British army in World War II, I made the first contacts with Jewish survivors in the death camps. I was called the _____.

9. I am the official term used for Jews who survived the Holocaust, wanted to leave Europe, but had nowhere to go because Western countries restricted immigration and the British limited immigration to Palestine. Call me _____.

10. I am the date on which the State of Israel was born. My four numbers are _____.

IDENTIFY THE ALIYAH*

To which aliyah does each of the following headlines or editorials refer? (An aliyah may be referred to more than once.)

1. Headline

HEBREW UNIVERSITY OFFICIALLY OPEN!
Big Ceremony at Mount Scopus!

_____

2. Editorial

"These young settlers live and work in a vacuum. Most of world Jewry has no idea that they even exist. There is no world-wide Zionist organization to support them or give them a sense of belonging. The Orthodox Jewish community has made them feel like godless interlopers. As for the Turkish authorities . . . well, let's not get into that now."

_____

3. Editorial

"What we have as a result of this aliyah is an instant, fully-formed professional class—doctors, lawyers, dentists, architects, professors, musicians, and the like."

_____

4. Headline

"BALFOUR'S ALIYAH" BRINGS BUMPER CROP OF PIONEERS!

_____

5. Headline

FIRST KEVUTZAH SET UP. SETTLERS DEDICATE THEMSELVES TO LABOR, SHARING, AND EQUALITY.

———————

6. Editorial

"'Hebrew vs. Yiddish,' that's all we hear nowadays. Ben Yehudah is a dedicated man with a brilliant vision; but so far his greatest achievement has been to tear the settlers apart."

———————

7. Headline

DISMAY OVER ARAB RIOTS! NEW IMMIGRANTS SAY, "WE FLED FROM VIOLENCE IN ONE LAND AND FIND IT IN ANOTHER."

———————

8. Editorial

"What is really thrilling is that the work of these ḥalutzim is starting to bear fruit. Look at the roads, the fields, and the communities they have built. Even the British are amazed. It seems that it was worth all the hardships, after all."

———————

9. Headline

"WE'RE ZIONISTS, NOT FARMERS," SAY NEW POLISH IMMIGRANTS.
Wave of Immigrants Swells Towns and Cities

———————

10. Editorial

"One of the first things that we must set up is some kind of self-defense group. We can't afford to leave our safety in the hands of Bedouin 'hired guns.' If the recent pogroms in Kishinev have taught us nothing else, they should have taught us that!"

———————

MAP PROJECT*

The chapter states, "Weizmann and Faisal were able to agree on the division of lands—it would be Arabia for the Arabs, Judea for the Jews." Where exactly was "Judea for the Jews" supposed to be? Using the chapter as your reference, draw a dotted line around the territory which the League of Nations designated as a Jewish state. "Arabia for the Arabs" is the rest of the land.

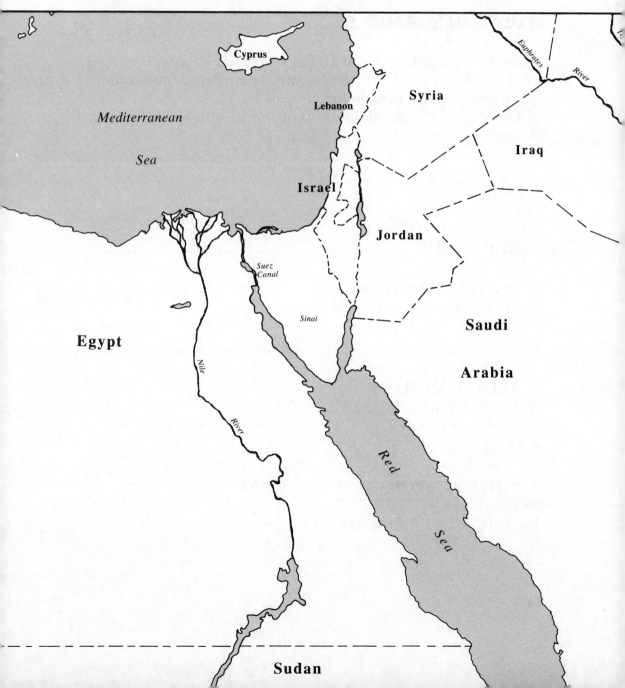

Chapter 22

THE NUCLEAR AGE

*A SLOGAN SCRAMBLE**

Since the end of World War II, the world has heard one slogan after another—some creative, some destructive, some noble, some greedy. Unscramble the slogans below to discover some of the ideas that have helped shape world history for the past 35 years.

1. POLITICAL
PEOPLE A TO
HAS INDEPENDENCE   ———————————————
EVERY RIGHT   ———————————————

2. ENTITLED UNDER
RIGHTS BLACKS TO
CIVIL ARE FULL LAW   ———————————————
THE   ———————————————

3. ALL GRANTED OF
WOMEN BE ALL MUST
IN EQUALITY LIFE   ———————————————
WALKS   ———————————————

4. THE DICTATORS
WORLD STAND THREATS
UP THE MUST FREE TO   ———————————————
OF   ———————————————

THEN AND TODAY

ON THE OTHER HAND . . .

Since these two statements were made at imaginary after-dinner speeches more than 30 years ago, things have changed. They were true statements when they were said, but there are reasons for thinking that things are a bit more confusing and complex today. Fill in the rest of the speech, beginning with the words "On the other hand."

1. "The atomic bomb has brought a swift and blessed end to the most destructive war in history. And in the future the power of the atom will be used for the good of all humanity."
   On the other hand . . .

2. "We are witnessing the end of the colonial empires in Asia and Africa. Now every people will have its own government. Every country will have the right to independence and self-determination."
   On the other hand . . .

SPECIAL PROJECT

AN ACTION PLAN

Dr. Martin Luther King, Jr. had much in common with Theodor Herzl. Both translated their dreams into action through organizing, persuading, dramatizing, and negotiating. Both paid careful attention to details. In short, they were both visionaries and activists. And King would have been comfortable with Herzl's saying, "If you will it, it is no dream."

To really change things, you have to have a plan for action. In the box at the left, put down something in your home, your neighborhood, your community, your synagogue, or your country that you would like to see changed. In the last box, put down the vision of change that you have in mind. Then, try to fill in logical steps that you could take to go from the first box to the last—from the problem to the dream.

PROBLEM (WHAT IS TO BE CHANGED)	STEPS					VISION (CHANGE FOR THE BETTER)
	1	2	3	4	5	

Chapter 23

THE STATE OF ISRAEL

A GENERAL REVIEW*

1. The name of the aliyah of Yemenite Jewry.

   _____

2. First stop of many immigrants to Israel in the early 1950s.

   _____

3. Nickname given to native-born Israelis and its meaning.

   _____

4. Israeli Arabs enjoy full rights of citizenship in Israel.   T   F

5. Christians and Moslems have more freedom of religion in Israel than do Conservative and Reform Jews.   T   F

6. Israel controls more territory today than it did in 1975.   T   F

7. Which of the following weapons have *not* been used (at one time or another) by the Arabs in their conflict with Israel?
   - (a) oil
   - (b) propaganda
   - (c) economic boycott
   - (d) terrorism
   - (e) political manipulation
   - (f) all-out war
   - (g) negotiations
   - (h) aircraft carriers

8. Circle the "outsider." The Palestinians   (a) were left largely deserted by other Arab nations for the best part of 20 years;   (b) made a mass exodus from Israel during the War of Independence;   (c) use terrorism with little concern for morality;   (d) have been supported by fellow Arabs since they

first sought a state of their own in 1936; (e) wish more than a simple military victory over Israel, but the total destruction of the Jewish state.

9. Which of the following Zionist goals has not been met?

(a) Jewish statehood

(b) revival of Hebrew

(c) reclamation of the land

(d) the end of anti-Semitism

(e) creation of new forms of social communities

(f) Israel as a home and haven for Jews

(g) Jews defending their own homeland

10. In which of the following ways do Israelis differ from their Arab neighbors?

(a) they speak a Semitic language

(b) they have many social and economic problems

(c) they are constantly in danger of war

(d) they belong to the United Nations

(e) they are threatened with national destruction

MAP STUDY*

Using the maps on page 211 of the textbook, answer the following questions:

1. Before the Six Day War, if the Israeli army had been forced to retreat it would have had no place to go. The battleground would have become the cities, towns, and villages of the Jewish state itself. T   F

2. Before the Six Day War, which Arab army could, by making a successful forward thrust, have cut the State of Israel in two?

_____

3. What Israeli port city was sandwiched between two Arab nations before the Six Day War? _____

4. Name the area, bordered by the Mediterranean Sea, which

has come to be known throughout the world as a center for Palestinean refugees—and which has served as a center for the launching of Arab terrorist raids against Israel? _____

5. Name the site, at the tip of the Sinai Peninsula, where the Israelis have set up a camp to insure that Israel will have a passage through the straits of Tiran into the Red Sea.

_____

6. One important benefit of Israel's victory in the Six Day War has been the advantages gained by the capture of the Sinai Peninsula, the West Bank, and the Golan Heights. Match the following advantages with one of the three areas. Write an S for Sinai, W for West Bank, and G for Golden Heights.

   (a) safe passage to the Red Sea   [   ]
   (b) borders that are straighter and easier to defend   [   ]
   (c) relief from artillery barrages for the villages and set-
       tlements in the Upper Galilee   [   ]
   (d) a united Jerusalem   [   ]
   (e) "cushions" of land area before a long and hard-to-
       defend border   [   ]

ISRAEL'S UNIQUENESS

The Four Questions we ask at the beginning of the Passover Seder might be used to help us focus on ways in which Israel is unique. Complete each of the following statements in your own words:

1. Whereas other states were created by people who have al-ways lived together in one place, Israel _____

_____

_____

2. Whereas most states have "national relatives," that is, they are linked to other states through language, culture, background, experience, or religion (for example, the United States and Canada, Spain and Italy which are both Catholic,

Mexico and Spain, etc.), Israel _____

_____

_____

3. Whereas other states are primarily involved with, and committed to, the people who live within their national borders, Israel _____

_____

_____

4. Whereas other states take their existence and survival for granted, Israel _____

_____

_____

THEN AND TODAY

PERSONAL IMPRESSIONS

1. Underline four words from the following list that express impressions you personally have about Israel today.

poor	fearful	isolated	industrious
courageous	different	suspicious	creative
Jewish		special	stubborn
endangered		a scapegoat	pioneering
a melting pot		a miracle	

2. Insert one of the four words you have chosen in the first blank of each sentence below, and complete the sentence.

    a. Israel is _____because

_____

_____

    b. Israel is _____because

_____

_____

_____

c. Israel is _____ because

_____

_____

_____

d. Israel is _____ because

_____

_____

_____

Chapter 24

MANY LANDS, ONE PEOPLE

COMMUNITY PROFILES*

Each statement below is true, except for one section that does not apply. Circle the section that is not true for the particular community.

1. The Jewish community in India   (a) extends back into the distant past;   (b) may have been visited by Rabbi David, brother of Maimonides;   (c) has withstood discrimination and at times life-threatening persecution without giving up its Jewish identity;   (d) has gone, in ever larger numbers, on aliyah to Israel.

2. The Jews of Trondheim, Norway   (a) are few in number compared to most Western congregations;   (b) were originally refugees from Russian pogroms;   (c) have the northernmost synagogue in the world;   (d) have very little to do with their Norwegian Gentile neighbors because they fear assimilation.

3. South African Jewry   (a) is leaving that country in great numbers today;   (b) is not harassed or persecuted by the government at this point;   (c) goes about its business with a good deal of caution because of the situation in that country;   (d) has a lifestyle pretty much like that of the Jewish community of the United States.

4. The Falashas   (a) believe that they are descended from King Solomon and the Queen of Sheba;   (b) live in conditions of extreme poverty and possible danger today;   (c) rejected the Talmud because it was written long after their ancestors settled in Ethiopia;   (d) were so isolated from the outside

world that, until the beginning of this century, they believed themselves to be the only Jews on earth.

5. Soviet Jews   (a) are one of the three largest Jewish populations on earth;   (b) prefer Yiddish to Hebrew or Russian, because it keeps them in touch with the world of their parents and grandparents;   (c) have put themselves in danger by declaring their desire to leave Russia in order to settle in Israel;   (d) have been singled out for special discrimination and persecution, unlike other religious groups in the Soviet Union.

6. Jews in Arab lands   (a) have experienced a long history of anti-Jewish policies and actions;   (b) have left their home countries, for the most part, to settle in Israel;   (c) are strictly forbidden to attend synagogue or organize religious schools;   (d) are often exposed to physical dangers, such as riots, by Muslim populations—particularly in times of war when feelings against Israel run high.

POSTMARKS*

These imaginary postcards come from a Jew who has been on a tour of Jewish communities around the world. On the basis of what each card says, fill in the postmark showing the country that was being visited.

_____

1. This is a very large, active, Jewish community, and I remember the hopes of Baron de Hirsch, but the anti-Semitism in this Latin metropolis is scary—the product of old-fashioned Catholicism and day-to-day political instability.

_____

2. Many of these people have gone on aliyah to Israel, but the stories remain along with the customs. What a fascinating way to give tzedakah. And I find the Hanukkah story the most exciting of all, for it shows how long this community has been around.

_____

3. Good, solid, middle-class people. Most of these Jews are active Zionists, too. But they are sitting on a powder keg, one

that's primed to explode any time now. It's a story told in black and white—and the Jews may end up in the middle.

_____

4. So near, and yet so far. It's maddening. A stone's throw from the Jewish state, and yet these poor Jews are forced to live in ghettos that seem right out of the Middle Ages. Labeled. Limited. With anti-Semitism all around them. I don't know if this postcard will get past the authorities and reach you, but I just had to write.

TRUE OR FALSE?* (T) (F)

1. The Indian Jews knew nothing of Ḥanukkah because their ancestors were shipwrecked and their Jewish books were lost at sea. T F

2. The Jews in Arab lands lived as equals with their neighbors and enjoyed full civil rights up until the outbreak of the War of Independence in 1948. T F

3. Gheez is a local language in which the Falasha Jews studied the Torah. T F

4. Moroccan and Tunisian Jews are protected by the government because their countries have preserved their civil rights. T F

5. Most of the Jews of the Arab world now live in Israel. T F

6. A "refusenik" is likely to meet a wide variety of problems set up by the government. T F

7. The Syrian government has gone to great lengths to make clear the difference between a Jew and a Zionist. T F

8. The Soviet Union has made a large effort on a number of fronts, over a period of many years, to destroy Jewish life within its borders. T F

SPECIAL PROJECT

SIMILARITIES

The chapter points out that "... the most striking thing is not the differences between these Jews, but their basic similarity." At the top of the chart are some key Jewish experiences and responses. To see whether or not Jewish communities around the world are similar, try filling in the chart with what you have studied in this chapter.

	A degree of isolation from other Jewish communities	Uncertainty and possible danger of persecution	Pressure to convert or abandon their Judaism	Special customs and rituals	Determination to remain Jewish
1. Falashas					
2. India's Jews					
3. Soviet Jews					
4. Jews in Arab lands					
5. Jews in Trondheim					
6. Jews of Argentina and South Africa					

105

Chapter 25

AMERICA SINCE WORLD WAR II

INSIGHTS IN DEPTH

Support each of the following general statements with a specific reference to, or a quotation from, the text:

1. There are things about modern American society which may disrupt, or even prove harmful to, Jewish aims and interests. _____

_____

_____

2. The more Jews came to feel at home in the United States, the more they were willing to express their Jewish identity.

_____

_____

3. America's Jews have shown deep concern, in words and in actions, for Jewish causes the world over. _____

_____

_____

_____

4. Just like the history of America in this century, American Jewish history has been in a state of constant change and great activity. _____

_____

_____

AN AMERICAN JEWISH PROBLEM FILE

Each file folder below details one problem threatening modern Jewish life in America. Using the chapter as a reference, fill in the definition of the problem, one or more of its major causes, what might be its results; and then, using your own imagination, give any idea you may have for solving the problem.

CONFIDENTIAL FILE #1
INTERMARRIAGE

Definition _____

_____

_____

Major cause(s) _____

_____

_____

Possible result(s) _____

_____

_____

Possible solution(s) _____

_____

_____

CONFIDENTIAL FILE #2
INSUFFICIENT JEWISH EDUCATION

Definition _____

_____

_____

Major cause(s) _____

_____

_____

Possible result(s) _____

_____

_____

Possible solution(s) _____

_____

_____

LOSS OF JEWISH IDENTITY—ASSIMILATION

Definition _____

_____

_____

Major cause(s) _____

_____

_____

Possible result(s) _____

_____

_____

Possible solution(s) _____

_____

_____

TODAY AND TOMORROW

A PERSONAL TIME CAPSULE

Time capsules are ways of reaching into the future. They give us a chance to tell our descendants how we feel about life today—and too, how we hope life will be in the future. Here is a chance to build a miniature personal "time capsule" made up of the Jewish elements of your life. Imagine, as you fill in the spaces below, that your time capsule will be opened by your great-great-grandchildren a hundred years from now.

1. My Jewish education

2. Ways in which my family observes its Judaism

3. What I like best about being Jewish

4. What bothers me the most about being Jewish

5. How I think Jewish life may be different in a hundred years

6. A few things about being Jewish that I hope will never change

Time capsules usually contain objects as well as writings. If you had to leave behind three things which might help your great-great-grandchildren understand Judaism as you understand it, what would you place in your time capsule?

1. _____

2. _____

3. _____

CROSSWORD

A VIEW OF AMERICAN JEWISH LIFE*

(Clue: All the people named in the puzzle are identified by their last name only. Good luck.)

Across

1. The first Jew to serve as a Supreme Court Justice; also, name of a university.
3. Cofounder of the American Red Cross.
4. Greatest Jewish catastrophe (in the minds of many, the greatest world catastrophe as well).
5. Pants named after a nineteenth century Jewish businessman who made his fortune in the rough-and-tumble territory of California during the Gold Rush.
8. Product of the electronic era, largely pioneered by immigrant and first-generation Jews—it revolutionized popular culture.
9. A Hall of Fame pitcher from the 1960s, who showed us that one can be both a great sports figure and a good Jew.

10. A development that poses an ever-growing threat to the American Jewish family.
11. An American Jewish labor union leader who, among his many achievements, made Labor Day a national holiday.
12. A major league slugger who came close to breaking one of Babe Ruth's home run records.

Down

1. An immigrant Jew who became one of America's greatest and most beloved songwriters.
2. A process of becoming a part of the country in which you live at the *expense* of your Jewish identity.
3. One of the great radio and television pioneers.
6. An informal, close-knit Jewish community.
7. A great Reform rabbi who

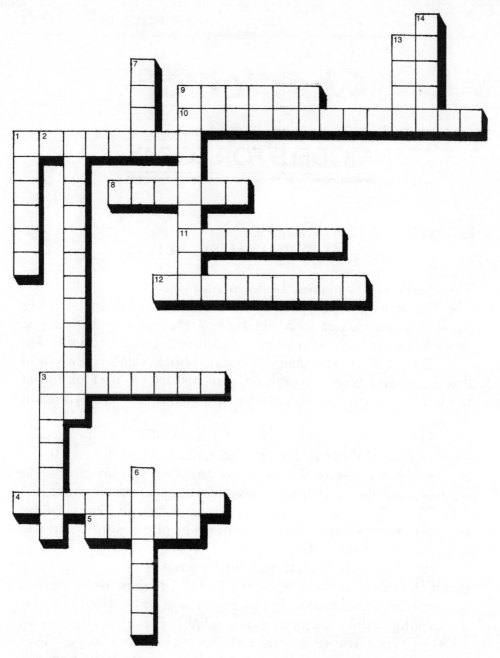

courageously addressed the social and moral issues of his day in his sermons.

9. The first Jewish Secretary of State in this country. He held office during the Yom Kippur War and played an important role in the development that followed.

13. An outgrowth of the American theater to which Jewish writers and composers have made a vast contribution.

14. A modern delicacy that might have had its roots in a food eaten by Jews on Pesah.

Chapter 26

MODELS FOR TODAY

CREATING A JEWISH LIFE
MY PERSONAL SEARCH

The final chapter makes the following points:

A. When we avoid trying to be Jewish we end up cheating ourselves out of our rich heritage, a way of life which has proved rewarding, and a sense of connection to our own roots.

B. Today there are many ways of being a good Jew—and this has been true throughout our history. A part of being Jewish has always been making choices about what Judaism means.

C. There is no single "way" of Jewish life. But Jews who have practiced their Judaism have usually shared two ideals: the search for a way for Judaism and the Jewish people to survive; and the search for a way to put Judaism into action.

D. Every Jew must seek his or her own special place "in the survival of our people, the development of our souls, and the betterment of humanity."

E. Judaism is more than just doing what is nice or right at a given moment. To be important to us, Judaism must have a bigger goal, a goal that helps us in our search for what is right.

Our long history helps us to see what Judaism has been, and tells us what Jews throughout the ages have hoped that Judaism might become. But what Judaism actually becomes is up to each of us—it is the result of each Jew's personal search for what Judaism means. Of course, the past has given us many clues by showing us the basic areas in which Judaism can operate.

Below are five areas of life in which Judaism and the Jewish people have special meaning. Ask yourself the question of the Jewish searcher: "What am I looking for in each of these areas?"

1. In my traditions and prayers?

2. In my Jewish studies?

3. In my family?

4. In my community?

5. In my relations with Israel?

To our continuing search—Shalom!

ANSWER KEY

This workbook has two kinds of questions: those that may be answered by reference to facts and data in the textbook; and those that require the student to interpret the material being studied in the light of his or her ideas. The following key provides answers *only* for those questions that are factual in nature.

Chapter 1

A JEWISH TRAVEL DIARY—1776 1. Frankfurt 2. Ethiopia 3. Jerusalem 4. Philadelphia 5. Rome 6. Shearith Israel 7. Berlin 8. Vilna, Poland **FIND THE OUTSIDER** 1. c 2. b 3. b 4. d 5. a 6. c **IDEA SCRAMBLE** 1. All men are created equal 2. Kings are not chosen by god 3. The ghetto walls must come crumbling down 4. The Jews must live as free citizens 5. People must make their own laws 6. All ideas must be examined by standards of reason 7. Freedom is an aim worth fighting for 8. A good Jew must pray with feeling

Chapter 2

WHO, OR WHAT, AM I? 1. Queen Isabella 2. Western Wall 3. Rabbi Haim Abulafia 4. Peter Stuyvesant 5. Rabbi Joseph Karo 6. Tzedakah 7. Haym Salomon 8. Asser Levy 9. Luis de Torres 10. John Adams **WORD SCRAMBLE** 1. Prejudice 2. Persecution 3. Hardship 4. Minority 5. Friendship 6. Understanding Circled letters: Opportunity **EVENTS AND EFFECTS** 5; 3; 4; 6; 1; 2 **JEWS ON THE MOVE** 1. Recife, Brazil 2. New Amsterdam 3. Massachusetts 4. Caribbean Sea 5. Newport, Rhode Island 6. Haifa 7. Jerusalem 8. Safed 9. Acre 10. Tiberias

Chapter 3

TRUE OR FALSE? 1. F 2. F 3. T 4. F 5. T 6. T 7. F 8. F 9. T 10. T 11. F 12. T **HUNTING HIDDEN WORDS** 1. Shtadlan 2. Baal Shem Tov 3. Tzedakah 4. Ketubah 5. Sanhedrin 6. Mitnagdim 7. Gaon

Chapter 4

WHO, WHAT, WHERE, AND WHEN AM I? 1. Venice 2. Moscow 3. *Communist Manifesto* 4. United States 5. Waterloo 6. Industrial Revolution 7. Nationalism 8. Socialism **IDEA SCRAMBLE** 1. The monarchy is an obsolete form of government 2. The rebellious common people must be put in their place 3. Europe can become a united empire 4. Every nation has a special character 5. Skilled craftsmen will be replaced by machines 6. The people have the right to constitutional government 7. Private industry has a right to make as much profit as it can 8. The workers must control the means of production

Chapter 5

FIND THE OUTSIDER 1. c 2. d 3. a 4. c 5. b 6. c **WORD SCRAMBLE** 1. Disloyal 2. Outsiders 3. Pushy 4. Different 5. Cheats

Chapter 6

TRUE OR FALSE? 1. T 2. T 3. F 4. T 5. F 6. F 7. T 8. F 9. T 10. T **SPEAKERS AND SERMONS** 1. Samson Raphael Hirsch 2. Samuel Holdheim 3. Heinrich Heine 4. Abraham Geiger 5. Zacharias Frankel 6. Leopold Zunz

Chapter 7

ACHIEVEMENTS AND AWARDS 1. Lionel de Rothschild 2. Daniel Mendoza 3. Sir Moses Montefiore 4. Nathan Mayer Rothschild 5. Gabriel Riesser 6. Ferdinand Lassalle 7. Adolphe Crémieux **AN OCCUPATION SCAN** (List these 7 words in whatever order you happen to find them.) 1. Philanthropist 2. Editor 3. Banker 4. Labor organizer 5. Lawyer 6. Boxer 7. Politician **A MEDIA MIX** 1. Daniel Mendoza becomes England's boxing champion 2. An editorial attack upon Ferdinand Lassalle 3. The abolition of the "Jewish Oath" in French Courts, as a result of Adolphe Crémieux's efforts. 4. The political and moral victory of Lionel de Rothschild, who is finally sworn into Parliament, *that body's first Jewish member* 5. The case of the Jewish boy who was kidnapped by the officers of the Pope, to be raised as a Christian 6. The "Damascus Affair"

Chapter 8

WHO, OR WHAT, AM I? 1. Rabbi Isaac Leeser 2. Rabbi Isaac Mayer Wise 3. Female Hebrew Benevolent Society 4. Peddling 5. Nathan Straus 6. Judah Touro **FIND THE OUTSIDER** 1. b 2. a 3. d 4. d 5. a 6. c **A JEWISH TOUR OF THE UNITED STATES IN THE NINETEENTH CENTURY** 1. Mississippi Valley 2. Philadelphia 3. Albany 4. Newport, Rhode Island 5. Mammoth Cave, Kentucky 6. Cincinnati 7. California Gold Rush area 8. New Orleans 9. New York City 10. Springfield, Illinois

Chapter 9

TRUE OR FALSE? 1. T 2. F 3. F (they were there many centuries before) 4. T 5. F 6. T 7. T 8. T **AN OVERVIEW** 1. odd facts, bizarre twists, and surprises 2. Christ-killers 3. in peace and mutual respect 4. monotheistic descendants 5. of any missionary effort on our part 6. our warm friendship 7. with the biggest Jewish state that ever was 8. our involvement in international trade 9. because of our contact with Jews in other countries 10. our real trouble began 11. all for law and order 12. of freedom and democracy 13. Russian czars and Jews should never mix 14. extension to the rule 15. in a class by himself 16. grand new heights of cruelty 17. in the name of God, and backed by the might of a nation 18. never to take security and well-being for granted 19. danger and darkness 20. our enemies' capacity to destroy us 21. the German Holocaust 22. hatred of and violence against them 23. one of the greatest communities in Jewish history **DIARIES AND DATES** 1. 1530 2. 50 B.C.E. 3. 1380 4. 1720 5. 810 6. 1797

Chapter 10

WHO, OR WHAT, AM I? 1. Ḥeder 2. Rabbi Levi Yitzḥok of Berdichev 3. Shabbat 4. Dowry 5. Shtetl 6. Melamed 7. Sholem Aleichem 8. Pilpul 9. Ḥabad 10. Musar **FIND THE OUTSIDER** 1. b 2. a 3. d 4. b 5. c **WORD SCRAMBLE** 1. Poverty 2. Piety 3. Family 4. Study 5. Danger 6. Closeness Circled letters: Tradition

Chapter 11

TRUE OR FALSE? 1. F 2. T 3. T 4. F 5. T 6. F 7. F

8. T 9. F 10. T **EVENTS AND EFFECTS** 5; 6; 1; 3; 2;
4 **"OPERATION DESTROY"** 1. Tax them to the point of poverty
2. Break up their communities 3. Deny them rights of citizenship
4. Take their children away from them 5. Confine them to a particular
territory 6. Encourage them to imitate their neighbors and to despise
their own identity

Chapter 12

MAP STUDY 1. Italy 2. Poland 3. Spain, Portugal, France,
Switzerland 4. Mediterranean Sea 5. Transjordan (known today as
Jordan) 6. Black Sea 7. Prussia and Bavaria **DIARIES AND
DATES** 1. 1800 2. 1916 3. 1880 4. 1860 5. 1900 6. 1919
HUNTING HIDDEN WORDS Colonialism Communism Zionism
Nationalism Nazism Militarism Socialism Imperialism

Chapter 13

PERSPECTIVES 1. the hopes and dreams 2. to divert the Russian
people 3. convenient scapegoats 4. most often organized and set into
motion by the government 5. students, writers, and members of the
middle class 6. sat on their hands 7. who dared to fight back
8. achieved unity, and worked together in harmony 9. lent legal
respectability 10. stripped of their rights as they were 11. how easily
and suddenly 12. in the role of helpless victim 13. there was no real
future for them 14. came to America 15. was at best an "iffy"
proposition 16. the Zionist idea 17. creating a Jewish homeland
WHO, WHAT, OR WHERE AM I? 1. Baron Edmond de Rothschild
2. *The Protocols of the Elders of Zion* 3. Menahem Mendel Beilis
4. Pogrom 5. May Laws 6. Kishinev 7. Haim Nahman Bialik
8. BILU (BILUIM)

Chapter 14

NEGATIVE HEADLINES AND COMMENTS 1. The pardon of Alfred
Dreyfus 2. The First Zionist Congress 3. The arrival in Palestine of the
First Aliyah, the BILU 4. The flight of Émile Zola 5. The publication
of Herzl's *The Jewish State* 6. The Uganda controversy, Sixth Zionist
Congress **A VALUE SCAN** Value 5 Responsibility for our own
defense is a cherished Zionist value, but it happens not to be expressed by
the history and idea of the little "Blue Box."

Chapter 15

FIND THE OUTSIDER 1. c 2. b 3. d 4. c 5. b **HUNTING HIDDEN WORDS** Newspaper education yiddish sweatshop union theater family shul **TESTIMONIALS** 1. Solomon Schechter 2. Baron de Hirsch 3. Samuel Gompers 4. Emma Lazarus 5. Abraham Golfaden

Chapter 16

A MEDIA MIX 1. The creation of the American Jewish Committee 2. The founding of the first Kevutzah (Deganiah) 3. The contribution of 200 million dollars, raised by the company of Jacob Schiff, to Japan during the Russo-Japanese War 4. The creation of the American Jewish Joint Distribution Committee 5. The vote of both houses of Congress in support of the American Jewish Committee's position, which resulted in this country's ending a long-standing trade agreement with Russia 6. The liberation of Jerusalem by the soldiers of Lord Allenby, including members of the Jewish Legion 7. The Balfour Declaration **WHO, WHAT, OR WHERE AM I?** 1. Bernard Baruch 2. Herbert Samuel 3. Petah Tikvah 4. Jacob Schiff 5. moshav **WORD SCRAMBLE** 1. Farming 2. Freedom 3. Equality 4. Sharing 5. Pioneering Circled letters: Redemption

Chapter 17

DIARIES AND DATES 1. 1935 2. 1920 3. 1938 4. 1946 5. 1940 6. 1932 **TRUE OR FALSE?** 1. F 2. T 3. T 4. F 5. T

Chapter 18

LOGICAL LESSONS 1. b 2. c 3. c 4. a 5. b **INDIVIDUALS AND THEIR IDEAS** 1. Mordecai Kaplan 2. Martin Buber 3. Louis Marshall 4. Charles A. Lindbergh 5. Franz Rosenzweig **IDEA SCRAMBLE** 1. International Jewry is plotting to take over the world 2. Judaism is a complete way of life 3. Jews must communicate with God on a personal basis 4. Modern problems can be examined from a traditional viewpoint 5. Jews must fight against restrictions of any kind

Chapter 19

IDENTIFY 1. Nuremberg Laws to the Jewish Problem 2. Master Race 3. Final Solution 4. Josef Goebbels 5. Book-burning 6. The Night of Broken Glass, *Kristalnacht* 7. Gypsies 8. Bergen-Belsen 9. Auschwitz 20. Yad Vashem **PHOTO EVIDENCE** Number 7. The Germans were equally cruel to *all* Jews **DIARIES AND DATES** 1. 1944 2. 1938 3. 1932 4. 1940 5. 1943

Chapter 20

TRUE OR FALSE? 1. T 2. F 3. F 4. T 5. F 6. T 7. F 8. T **THE RESISTANCE** 1. c 2. a 3. b 4. c 5. b **INDIVIDUALS AND THEIR ACHIEVEMENTS** 5; 4; 1; 2; 3; 1; 4

Chapter 21

WHO, OR WHAT, AM I? 1. Emir Faisal 2. Sir Herbert Samuel 3. Havlagah, or self-restraint 4. Transjordan (known today as the Kingdom of Jordan) 5. riots 6. France 7. White Paper 8. Jewish Brigade 9. Displaced Persons 10. May 14, 1948, or the 6th of Iyar, 5708 **MAP PROJECT** "Judea for the Jews" included what is known today as Israel and Jordan **IDENTIFY THE ALIYAH** 1. Fourth Aliyah 2. First Aliyah 3. Fifth Aliyah 4. Third Aliyah 5. Second Aliyah 6. First Aliyah 7. Fifth Aliyah (and a case can be made as well for the Fourth Aliyah, responding to the smaller riots of 1929) 8. Third Aliyah 9. Fourth Aliyah 10. Second Aliyah

Chapter 22

A SLOGAN SCRAMBLE 1. Every people has a right to political independence 2. Blacks are entitled to full civil rights under the law 3. All women must be granted equality in all walks of life 4. The free world must stand up to the threats of dictators

Chapter 23

A GENERAL REVIEW 1. Operation Magic Carpet 2. Maabarot
3. Sabra—like the fruit of the Sabra cactus: tough on the outside, but sweet
on the inside 4. T 5. T 6. F 7. h 8. d 9. d 10. e **MAP
STUDY** 1. T 2. Jordan 3. Elat 4. Gaza 5. Sharm el Sheikh
6a. S 6b. W 6c. G 6d. W 6e. S

Chapter 24

COMMUNITY PROFILES 1. c 2. d 3. a 4. c 5. b 6. c
POSTMARKS 1. Argentina 2. India 3. South Africa 4. Syria
TRUE OR FALSE? 1. F 2. F 3. T 4. T 5. T 6. T 7. F 8. T

Chapter 25

A VIEW OF AMERICAN JEWISH LIFE *Across:* 1. Brandeis
3. Solomons 4. Holocaust 5. Levis 8. Movies 9. Koufax
10. Intermarriage 11. Gompers 12. Greenberg

Down: 1. Berlin 2. Assimilation 3. Sarnoff 6. Havurah 7. Wise
9. Kissinger 13. Musicals 14. Pizza